GREEN GOLDFISH 2.0

15 KEYS TO DRIVING EMPLOYEE ENGAGEMENT

STAN PHELPS
&
LAUREN MCGHEE

PRAISE FOR
GREEN GOLDFISH 2.0

"In a time when company vision and culture matter more than ever, it takes inspired and engaged employees to bring them to life."

- BRIAN SOLIS, AUTHOR OF *WHAT'S THE FUTURE OF BUSINESS #WTF*, *THE END OF BUSINESS AS USUAL*, AND *ENGAGE!*

"So often overlooked, and so very vital to building company value... empowering employees to support each other and the brand. *Green Goldfish 2.0* will walk you step-by-step though achieving this critical goal."

- TED RUBIN, AUTHOR OF *RETURN ON RELATIONSHIP*

"*Green Goldfish 2.0* shows how to manage employees by commitment and not control. Bravo!"

- BARRY MOLTZ, AUTHOR OF *BAM, BOUNCE*, AND *GETTING BUSINESS UNSTUCK*

"*Green Goldfish 2.0* takes customer service to a whole new level by focusing on EMPLOYEE service, and how to do well by your employees - so they take care of your customers. Packed with stories, insights and R.U.L.E.S. any company can follow, this book is a must-read for managers of companies of all shapes and sizes who know that employees don't leave jobs—they leave managers, especially when they don't feel your love and appreciation. Pick this up, and start engaging your team and making more GREEN!

- PHIL GERBYSHAK, AUTHOR OF *THE NAKED TRUTH OF SOCIAL MEDIA*

"If you're looking for ways to inspire your employees to love your company, and if you're smart enough to realize that money can't buy you love, then you need real-life, uber-successful examples from real-life, uber-profitable companies. Look no farther! In your hands, you've got examples from hundreds and hundreds of companies."

- TED COINÉ, AUTHOR OF *FIVE STAR CUSTOMER SERVICE* *AND SPOIL'EM ROTTEN!*

"Our large-scale research shows unequivocally that engaged employees are more likely to work longer, try harder, make more suggestions for improvement, recruit others to join their company, and go out of their way to help customers. They even take less sick time. Companies can tap into the enormous value of engaged employees by following the 15 ideas laid out in this book."

- BRUCE TEMKIN, AUTHOR OF *THE SIX LAWS OF CUSTOMER EXPERIENCE*

Published by 9 INCH Marketing

Editing by Lee Heinrich of Write Way Publishing and layout by Evan Carroll.

ISBN: 978-1-7326652-2-4

First Printing: 2018

Printed in the United States of America

Green Goldfish 2.0 is available for bulk orders. For further details and special pricing, please e-mail: stan@purplegoldfish.com or call +1.919.360.4702

This book is dedicated to the memory of my mother,
Pauline Dora Phelps. The first person to believe
in me and encourage me to follow my dreams
no matter the cost.

—Stan Phelps

This book is dedicated to my best friend, my rock,
my husband, Tyler McGhee. Thank you for your relentless
support and for seeing more in me than I ever could.

—Lauren McGhee

CONTENTS

FOREWORD

BY TED COINÉ

*"No, a Green Goldfish does not have to cost your
company a single penny. It isn't about the money.
You can't buy your employees' love, no matter how
much you spend. But you sure can invest in it, as the
examples in this book attest."*

For years now, I've been sharing a basic truth with my audiences and readers: *In business, doing the right thing pays.* You can call this good karma or following the Golden Rule if you choose. For those of you who are more pragmatic, you can chalk it up to savvy business sense. Whether you're focused on the first half of this proposition (*doing the right thing*) or the second (*pays*), my role is to drive this message home in a way my print and real-life audiences can taste, feel, and ultimately buy into. Because let's face it: you can tell someone the truth until your throat is raw. Until they own it for themselves, you're wasting your time and theirs.

Fortunately, even the most intelligent of us humans respond well to two types of new information: that which is simple and real-life examples.

So, imagine my delight when my friend Stan Phelps began his Goldfish projects years ago! It seemed like every day he would post on his blog a new example of little things that make a world of difference. He set out to collect 1,001 examples and asked his robust social media network for help.

The results of this initial (brilliantly crowdsourced) research are available in his first book, *Purple Goldfish*. Chances are good you've already read it, and you're back now for a deeper dive.

"Deeper?" Absolutely. *Purple Goldfish* is all about customer service. Stan's premise is simple and, to anyone who's owned or run a business, inescapable: spoil your customers rotten, surprise them with a little extra that they can't get anywhere else, and they're yours for life. Better, their friends will be, too, because there's nothing we humans enjoy more than sharing stories—good or bad—with our friends. Give your customers an irresistible story to share about how wonderful your company is, and they'll become your most effective sales force. The *Purple Goldfish Project* provides 1,001 such stories, about almost as many companies.

So that's his *Purple Goldfish* book, and if you haven't read it, read it next. But I claim this *Green Goldfish 2.0* book—this one—takes you one deeper. Here's how:

With the right practices in place, with good training and tight-as-a-drum supervision, even the most draconian of managements can achieve winning customer service that wows customers. I hate to admit that, but I've seen it with my own eyes, so I have to be honest. Fortunately, it's beyond rare that a company can pull this off. It's just too exhausting to maintain with any consistency. Customers can sense employee misery, even through forced smiles, and it turns them off.

What turns customers *on* is sincerity: employee *love* of their company—engagement, in other words. That is where the *Green Goldfish 2.0* book comes in—yes, the one you are holding in your hands right now!

If you're looking for ways to inspire your employees to love your company, and if you're smart enough to realize that money can't buy you love, then you need real-life, uber-successful examples from real-life, uber-profitable companies. Look no farther! In your hands, you've got examples from hundreds and hundreds of companies. Some are firms you already know. For instance:

- **Facebook** gives employees a bonus for having a baby—just when they need it most!

- **Patagonia** makes the world—and employees' lives—better through two weeks of paid time off to work in the green non-profit of their choice.

- **Intel** has greeters and gifts awaiting new hires. What a way to start a new career!

Others are ones you've likely never heard of, but they are worth getting to know well, including:

- **Realflow** who engages employees through smoothie competitions. Taste and healthy ingredients are included in judging criteria.

- **Tarbar** with their Thumbs Up Award which is a roaming, desktop statue employees can earn by doing something above and beyond the call of job performance.

- **AnswerLab** employees can each schedule one-on-one time with their CEO to "walk and talk"—literally. He goes for a walk with each one!

If you notice, some of these Green Goldfish companies invest green—that is, money—in ways that show their employees how important they are to the company. The first three examples all fit into this category. A little bit of money, invested meaningfully, can indeed get your point across quite well.

But if you also notice, you don't have to spend a dime in order to get this message through (and as a pathologically frugal former CEO myself, this really works for me!). How much do smoothie ingredients cost? How much does one roaming award cost?

And my favorite of the list, the walk and talk with the CEO—last time I checked, walking was free. Free, but priceless! As most readers of my blog, SwitchandShift.com, are well aware, I have a special place in my heart—and in most posts—for the power of Management by Walking Around: and the more casual the walking (or eating), the more likely important, company-improving issues will bubble to the top where something can be done about them.

No, a Green Goldfish does not have to cost your company a single penny. It isn't about the money. Green Goldfish—and the green of profits—they're all about employee engagement, employee love. You can't buy your employees' love, no matter how much you spend. But you sure can invest in it, as the 200+ examples in this book attest.

I'd like to close this foreword with a quote from an employee at another of the Green Goldfish companies, SAS Institute, "You're given the freedom, the flexibility, and the resources to do your job. Because if you're treated well, you treat the company well." Doing the right thing pays. *Green Goldfish 2.0* is your how-to manual to make this essential business truth come to life at your company. Buy it. Read it. Share it. Most importantly, do it.

You'll thank me for this advice. You'll thank Stan Phelps and Lauren McGhee for this book.

— Ted Coiné
Former CEO, Speaker, and Business Heretic
Author of *Five Star Customer Service* and *Spoil'em Rotten*

INTRODUCTION

BY STAN PHELPS

"I came to see in my time at IBM that 'culture' isn't just one aspect of the game – it is the game."

— Lou Gerstner, Former IBM CEO, Author of *Who Says Elephants Can't Dance*

HAPPY EMPLOYEES CREATE
HAPPY CUSTOMERS

In 2012, I completed a quest. I had set out to find 1,001 Purple Goldfish—examples of companies that strive to exceed customer expectations via a sticky concept called **g.l.u.e.** (giving little unexpected extras). Signature extras that help win customers and influence word of mouth.

What became clear during my research is that most brands who practice marketing g.l.u.e. for customers also embrace the same concept with employees. Taking care of employees and investing in the "little extras" for staff helps build a dynamic, healthy culture.

Here is a great quote by Vince Burks of Amica Insurance explaining this exact focus:

> The concept of lagniappe is not just a part of our brand ethos; it is ingrained in everything we do. It therefore extends to our most valued resource—our employees. In fact, that is the secret to our success. Excellent benefits. Advancement opportunities. The latest technology. A real work/life balance. And an open and regular line of communication with each other and with senior management. Taken together, we give our employees all that they need to succeed...and more. This is absolutely essential. Satisfied employees lead to satisfied customers. Long-term employees lead to long-term relationships with customers. And pride, trust, and morale are all contagious. Further, well-trained, long-term employees know how to get the job done quickly, efficiently, and effectively. They know their customers. They know their colleagues. They know their company. And they therefore know how to 'get

to yes' with ease and a sense of grace. This is good for
the customer. This is good for the company.

Satisfied employees do indeed lead to satisfied customers. This
book is an update to the second book in the Goldfish Series, *What's
Your Green Goldfish?* The original was based on a collection of 1,001
examples of little extras for employees. Why is green symbolic for
employees? Here are three important reasons:

1. **NOLA** - Green is one of the three colors of Mardi Gras (purple,
   green and gold). New Orleans is the birthplace of lagniappe,
   the overarching concept for "giving little unexpected extras" for
   employees.

2. **Beyond Dollars:** The second reason deals with money. Studies
   show financial compensation is not a strong long-term motivator for employees. Money can be more of a hindrance than a
   help.

3. **Growing**: Green is about growth. When you are green, you
   are growing. When you are ripe, you begin to rot. Green Goldfish are the little things that can make the big difference in establishing culture.

Similar to a Purple Goldfish, it is my belief that a Green Goldfish
provides three benefits:

1. **Differentiation**. Doing little extras provide a tangible way to
   stand out in a sea of sameness. The little extra gives the company a "remark"able difference or set of signature differences.

2. **Retention**. If you keep employees happy, they tend to stick
   around longer.

3. **Word of mouth**. By creating a culture that attracts talent, you can become a desired place to work. The result is that you'll get more "A" players.

2.0 EDITION

In 2017, I met Lauren McGhee outside the building of a co-working space. I was on the phone speaking to someone about employee engagement and apparently Lauren was eavesdropping. Once I hung up the phone, she strolled down the sidewalk to introduce herself. Thus began our relationship. Lauren is a Gallup-certified Strengths-Finder coach and speaker. We interact often through PRiSM Speakers[1], a speaker group based in the Research Triangle Park. Her core belief is that everyone should thrive in the workplace. She believes in the power of purposeful design. That companies can leverage individual and team strengths in action to promote increased employee engagement. As a millennial herself, Lauren has a personal interest in how millennials function in the workplace. We decided to collaborate on an updated version of *What's Your Green Goldfish?* The 2.0 version was born.

Green Goldfish 2.0 is broken into four main sections:

Section I: Here we outline the Why. This part of our book explores the reasons for focusing on engagement and where the metaphor of a Goldfish originated.

Section II: This is where we explore the Ingredients. We'll uncover the five R.U.L.E.S. for creating a Green Goldfish: Relevant, Unexpected, Limited, Expressive and Sticky.

---

1. http://prismspeakers.com

Section III: We uncover the What in this section. Here we share the 15 different types of Green Goldfish and the categories they fall under: the three B's: Building, Belonging, and Becoming.

Section IV: Closing it out. We share five final thoughts and offer suggestions for additional reading.

Ready to jump in and learn how to create your own Green Goldfish? We'll start with two stories that underscore the importance of engagement. Let's go ...

PROLOGUE

"Our people are our single greatest strength and most enduring long-term competitive advantage."

— Gary Kelly, Southwest Airlines CEO

TOWELS & HAMMERS:
A TALE OF TWO GIANTS

In 2011, **Google** was crowned the "Happiest Company in America" by CareerBliss.com. The rankings are based on 100,000+ worker-generated reviews spanning over 10,000 companies. Scores were based on such factors as work-life balance, relationships with bosses and co-workers, compensation, growth opportunities, a company's culture, and the opportunity for employees to exert control over the daily workflow.

Google didn't become a happy company by mistake. It's a product of thoughtful design and ultimately, culture. Founders Larry Page and Sergey Brin set the groundwork for building Google. Here are some telling quotes by CEO Page in a *New York Times* post:

> We have somewhat of a social mission, and most other companies do not. I think that's why people like working for us, and using our services .... Companies' goals should be to make their employees so wealthy that they do not need to work, but choose to because they believe in the company .... Hopefully, I believe in a world of abundance, and in that world, many of our employees don't have to work, they're pretty wealthy and they could probably go years without working. Why are they working? They're working because they like doing something, they believe in what they're doing.[2]

But maybe there is a deeper reason for creating a more welcoming and fulfilling workplace. Here is a quote from CEO Page's Commencement Address at the University of Michigan in May 2009 (YouTube video):

---

2. http://bits.blogs.nytimes.com/2012/10/17/larry-page-on-regulation-maps-and-googles-social-mission/

My father's father worked in the Chevy plant in Flint, Michigan. He was an assembly line worker. My Grandpa used to carry an "Alley Oop" hammer—a heavy iron pipe with a hunk of lead melted on the end. The workers made them during the sit-down strikes to protect themselves. When I was growing up, we used that hammer whenever we needed to pound a stake or something into the ground. It is wonderful that most people don't need to carry a heavy blunt object for protection anymore. But just in case, I have it here.[3]

Source: YouTube

It bears repeating. **Larry Page's grandfather used to take a hammer to work for protection**. A lead pipe with a hunk of metal melted on the end of it. I can only imagine this was a constant reminder of the quest for a happy workplace at Google.

---

3. https://www.youtube.com/watch?v=qFb2rvmrahc

THROWING IN THE TOWELS

As part of a broad series of cutbacks in 2004, Microsoft eliminated the laundered towel service. The towels were available for employees who showered after biking to work or playing sports on the company's Redmond campus. That and the other changes, especially to the employee stock purchase program, caused a groundswell of opposition from Microsoft employees, folks commonly referred to as "Softies." The towels became a rallying point of discontent.[4]

According to the blog mini Microsoft, "It's not like we're sweaty work-out animals always in need of a shower and fresh towel. No. What riled us was the bone-headed way the towel cut-back was handled, explained, and justified. It truly made us wonder just who are these people in charge and just who do they think they are leading? The towels became the symbol of poor leadership."

Rancor continued and some prominent departures from Microsoft ensued. *Business Week* reported about troubling exits, "Just whisper the word 'towels' to any Microsoft employee, and eyes roll. Employees who helped the company build its huge cash stockpile were furious."[5]

Less than two years later, the towels were back. Microsoft reinstated the laundered towel service and even added some extras in an effort to stem the tide of exits and to increase morale.

---

4. https://www.seattlepi.com/business/article/Grumbling-at-Microsoft-grows-1145655.php
5. http://www.businessweek.com/stories/2005-09-25/troubling-exits-at-microsoft

PREFACE

*"It is our belief that work/life balance should be
in the hands of the employee and that
happy, balanced people make better employees."*

— Janelle Raney, Citrix

THE WORKPLACE IS CHANGING

One could make the assertion that "workplace" has changed more in the last five years than it has in the previous twenty-five. Seismic shifts in technology, social media, and management have drastically changed how we work. Pair this with the Gallup report in December 2017 that 85 percent of employees worldwide are not engaged or are actively disengaged at work, and there is clearly a recognizable need to ignite employee engagement.[6]

Let's look at 10 compelling reasons to invest in employee engagement:

10. DOLLARS AND SENSE

- If organizations increased investment in a range of good workplace practices related to engagement by just 10 percent, they would increase profits by $2,400 per employee.[7]

- Fewer than one in 10 middle managers deemed the quality of their management training to be excellent.[8]

- According to Gallup statistics, only 14 percent of employees strongly agree that their performance reviews inspire them to actually improve.[9]

6. https://www.gallup.com/workplace/231668/dismal-employee-engagement-sign-global-mismanagement.aspx

7. https://talentculture.com/6-eye-opening-employee-engagement-statistics/

8. https://www.accenture.com

9. https://www.gallup.com/workplace/236135/give-performance-reviews-actually-inspire-employees.aspx

9. PEOPLE ARE PEOPLE

Engagement and involvement are critical in managing change at work; nine out of 10 of the key barriers to the success of change programs are people related.[10]

- Employees need hope to be engaged. Gallup says that 69 percent of people who strongly agreed that their leaders made them feel enthusiastic and hopeful about the future were engaged. For those who strongly disagreed, only one percent of them were engaged at work.[11]

8. TRIPLE YOUR PLEASURE

- Engaged organizations grew profits as much as three times faster than their competitors. Highly engaged organizations have the potential to reduce staff turnover by 87 percent and improve performance by 20 percent.[12]

7. HORRIBLE BOSSES

- 75 percent of people voluntarily leaving jobs don't quit their jobs; they quit their bosses.[13]

- A *Harvard Business Review* report states that 58 percent of people say they would trust a stranger more than their actual boss.[14]

---

10. https://www.slideshare.net/businessandthegeek/human-resources-employee-engagement-statistics
11. http://coaching.gallup.com/2015/10/the-four-things-followers-need-and-how.html
12. https://news.cebglobal.com/press-releases?item=67169
13. http://www.thesocialworkplace.com/2011/08/08/social-knows-employee-engagement-statistics-august-2011-edition/
14. https://www.forbes.com/sites/davidsturt/2018/03/08/10-shocking-workplace-stats-you-need-to-know/#2b20e204f3af

6. IS IT IGNORANCE OR APATHY?

- I don't know and I don't care. Roughly 67 percent of employees fall in the "not engaged" column, 15 percent fall in the "engaged" category, meaning about 18 percent are "actively disengaged." Gallup thinks that the apathetic or "not engaged" people are those that businesses should worry about most.[15]

5. WHAT'S YOUR RETURN ON ENGAGEMENT?

- Fewer than 50 percent of Chief Financial Officers appear to understand the return on their investments in human capital.[16]

4. SHOW ME THE PLAN

- Based on a recent study by Chris Zook, only 40 percent of the workforce knew about the corporation's goals, strategies, and tactics.[17]

3. RECOGNITION MATTERS

- Forty-three percent of highly engaged employees receive feedback at least once a week compared to only 18 percent of employees with low engagement.[18]

2. MOVING THE NEEDLE

- Based on the earnings per share (EPS) growth of 89 organizations, it was noted that the EPS growth rate of organizations

15. http://rapidbi.com/howtowriteaninternalcommunicationsplanandstrategy/

16. https://www.accenture.com/t20180910T083815Z__w__/us-en/_acnmedia/PDF-85/Accenture-CFO-Research-Global.pdf

17. https://www.amazon.com/Socialized-Successful-Businesses-Harness-Century/dp/1937134431

18. https://temenosinc.com/resources/white-papers/employee-feedback/

with engagement scores in the top quartile were 2.6 times that of organizations with below-average engagement scores.[19]

... and the #1 reason for paying attention to employee engagement:

1. SINCERITY AND TRUST

- Of seventy-five possible drivers of engagement the **ONE** that was rated as the most important was the extent to which employees believed that their senior management had a sincere interest in their well-being.[20]

19. https://blog.cultureamp.com/engaging-to-earn-3-ways-engaged-employees-boost-the-bottom-line

20. https://www.gallup.com/workplace/236483/enhances-benefits-employee-engagement.aspx

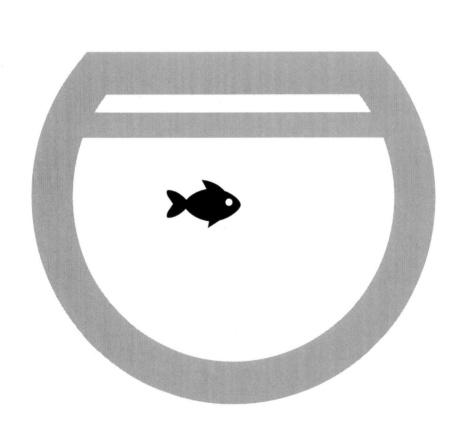

PART 1:

WHAT IS A GREEN GOLDFISH?

CHAPTER 1

EMPLOYEE FIRST

"Employees First, Customers Second
is a management approach.
It is a philosophy, a set of ideas, a way of looking
at strategy and competitive advantage."

— Vineet Nayar, Former CEO HCL Technologies

THE MOST IMPORTANT
TWO FEET IN BUSINESS

Where is value created in an enterprise? It's created in the last two feet of a transaction—the space between the employee and the customer. In 2005, HCL Technologies of India needed a transformational change. New CEO Vineet Nayar decided to make a statement. He set out a new strategy focusing on "Employees First."

Vineet understood the importance of interactions between frontline employees and the customer. He calls these 24 inches the "value zone." The priority at HCL became: Employees first, customers second, management third, and shareholders last. His employees on the front line were the key to the HCL turnaround. They were the true custodians of the brand and drivers of customer loyalty. Nayar wanted to shift the focus from the "WHAT" of what HCL offered to the "HOW" of delivering value.

HCL decided to turn conventional management upside down. They inverted the pyramid and placed employees first. This wasn't just lip service. Vineet engaged in a number of changes that reinforced the new direction. It was a strategy that Vineet called "Blue Ocean Droplets." Inspired by the book *Blue Ocean Strategy*,[21] these droplets are the tangible changes on the journey. They are beacons along the voyage. They help drive employee engagement and reinforce culture. Nayar drew his inspiration from Mahatma Gandhi and his famous Dandi March. Mahatma walked to the sea to make salt as a protest to the British government about their monopoly on salt production in India. This small action ignited change, becoming a catalyst that led to a large-scale uprising.

Nayar knew he needed actions and not words. Here are some of the Green Goldfish changes HCL Technologies made on their journey:

---

21. https://www.blueoceanstrategy.com/what-is-blue-ocean-strategy/

OPENING THE WINDOW OF INFORMATION

HCL put together an online forum for employees called U&I. Employees could ask any question to the senior team at HCL Technologies. It was an open site where everyone could see the question, the questioner, and the answer. Employees responded favorably as noted by this comment: "This is the biggest change we have seen at HCL in years. Now we have a management team that is willing to acknowledge the dirt."

Why open the window of information? Vineet uses the analogy of an Amsterdam Window.[22] Having previously lived on the Herengracht ("Gentleman's Canal") in Amsterdam, Stan can attest that these windows are immense. They are a throwback to the modest Calvinist period when subtle expressions of wealth, such as being able to afford to pay the highest window tax, were favored by the rich. In the words of writer Joanna Tweedy, "Today, the centuries-old glass, beautifully imperfect, frames the olive-green waters outside and lets the natural light and the eyes of curious tourists pour in."

While visiting Amsterdam, Vineet pointed to windows and asked his friend, "Why so large?" The friend mentioned all the obvious reasons like letting in light and enjoying the view of the canal, but then offered a much more interesting answer. "It keeps the house clean." It turns out that the bigger your windows, the more glass you have, the more visible your dirt will be—to you and to everyone who visits or passes by.

In Vineet's words, "If you can see the dirt, you will be much more likely to get rid of it. A transparent house has a dramatic effect on the culture inside."

---

22. http://parisinnovationreview.com/articles-en/the-inverse-pyramid-of-vineet-nayar

TRUST PAY

Vineet developed a clear point of view on compensation and recognition during his twenty years with HCL. The industry used to pay 30 percent variable compensation to employees, linked to the company's performance. He found the idea quite ridiculous because if you are a software engineer, you have no meaningful influence on the performance of the company. So HCL turned that amount into fixed pay—"trust pay." It allowed HCL to start focusing on the value employees were creating for the customer."

OPEN 360-DEGREE REVIEW

To help invert the organizational pyramid, **HCL** opened the 360-degree performance review process to all employees whom a manager might influence and allowed anyone who had given a manager feedback access to the results of that manager's 360. This practice increased participation, empowered employees, and made the 360-review a development tool, not an evaluative one.[23]

TAKEAWAY

Culture trumps strategy, and principles beat rules. The entire premise of *Green Goldfish 2.0* is that employees must come first. Employee experience should be a priority for leadership.

---

23. https://www.amazon.com/s?k=9780544631601&i=stripbooks&linkCode=qs

CHAPTER 2

BUILDING THE FOUNDATION FOR RETENTION

"One thing that always surprised me in prior work experiences is when your assets walk out the door each day, why aren't companies doing more to value the people doing the business?"

— Robert Murray, CEO iProspect, Former Analyst Bain & Co

WHO IS MORE IMPORTANT?

This is a great chicken and egg question with regard to leadership. Who comes first? Customers or employees? What became clear during Stan's research is that brands who understand the concept of lagniappe for customers also embrace the concept with employees. Both are equally important. Taking care of employees and investing in the "little extras" for staff help build a dynamic culture.

WHAT TYPE OF COMPANY DO YOU WANT TO BE WHEN YOU GROW UP?

Some years ago, Stan crossed paths with a friend from college. They both had lived on the same floor their freshman year at Marist College. Tom captained the football team, brandishing a personality and a warm smile that lit up a room.

Tom was now a successful businessman, owning his own agency. Coyne Public Relations was based in Parsippany, New Jersey, and boasted an impressive list of clients. Tom and his team have worked with iconic brands such as Disney, Campbell Soup, and Burger King.

While sitting down with Tom, Stan had the opportunity to ask him about his business philosophy. Tom relayed an approach that was both simple and prophetic. In Tom's words, "When I started the agency, my goal was not to be the biggest or to have the best clients. It was simply to become the best agency to work for. I knew if we were the best agency to work for, we would then attract the best people. And that if we retained the best people, the best clients would follow."

It's been over two decades since Tom Coyne started his agency as a sole proprietor. The firm now boasts over 160 employees and maintains offices in both Parsippany and New York City. Coyne has been named the "Best Agency to Work for in America" by *The Holmes Report.*[24]

HOW DOES COYNE FOCUS ON BECOMING THE BEST?

Coyne focuses on putting its employees first, supporting employees by promoting a work/life balance and allowing team members not only to make a great living but also to enjoy a strong quality of life. The best companies like Coyne PR are places where employees are truly excited about coming in every day.

Here are some Green Goldfish from Coyne:

- Coyne College is the agency's internal training program. The program is designed to develop the knowledge and skills of Coyne's employees and give them the best opportunity to succeed wherever their careers take them. Beyond Coyne College, the agency encourages employees to seek additional ways to continue their education and further their understanding of public relations and their clients' industries.

- As part of designing the new offices at Coyne PR's HQ in New Jersey, the senior team polled the employees for suggestions. The result: The Zen Den, a room for relaxation. It's painted totally black and has massage chairs and a fish tank video screen. It's a perfect place to unwind and rejuvenate.

- Coyne has a nail salon in its office. Once a week it's open for employees free of charge.

---

24. https://www.coynepr.com/news-article/coyne-named-finalist-for-the-holmes-reports-north-american-midsize-pr-agency-of-the-year/

- Winter Fridays. In lieu of a formal company holiday party, Coyne PR recently decided to focus on employees for the entire month of December. One of the favorite activities was Winter Fridays. The entire firm received Fridays off for the month of December. On December 12, the agency surprised everyone by shuttling the whole agency over to the mall mid-morning. Each employee was given $250 to spend with one condition. The money needed to be spent on only themselves. All costs for food and beverages at the mall were covered. Employees could go anywhere they pleased and just drop their business card for payment. The day ended back at Coyne PR headquarters for food and drinks for the entire staff.

SHIFTING YOUR MINDSET

Employees are the bedrock of your organization. You would be better served taking compensation out of the equation and thinking of them as volunteers. Here is a great analysis from Ted Coiné on this exact approach:

> CEOs, team leaders, and everyone in between: if your people don't love your company after four years of employment (or four months, or four quarters), that's all on you .... Do you have the pick of the employment litter? Are your best people dying to stay on board? If not, it isn't that they're ungrateful, and it isn't that your competitors are luring them away. It's that you suck as a leader.... Act as if every single employee is a volunteer. Because you know what? In a fundamental way, they are.

TAKEAWAY

Focus on what you can control—creating a great work environment. That environment or culture will then attract the best people.

CHAPTER 3

WHY GREEN AND WHY A GOLDFISH?

"It has long been an axiom of mine that the little things are infinitely the most important."

— Sir Arthur Conan Doyle

GOLDFISH ON THE BRAIN

The origin of the goldfish dates back to 2009. It has become a signature part of this book series. The goldfish represents something small, but despite its size, it's something with the ability to make a big difference.

The first part of the inspiration for the goldfish came from Kimpton Hotels. The boutique hotel chain introduced something new in 2001. The Kimpton Hotel Monaco began to offer travelers the opportunity to adopt a temporary travel companion for their stay. Perhaps you are traveling on business and getting a little lonely. Or maybe you are with family and missing your family pet. Kimpton to the rescue; they will give you a goldfish for your stay. They call the program Guppy Love.

"The 'Guppy Love' program is a fun extension of our pet-friendly nature as well as our emphasis on indulging the senses to heighten the travel experience," says Steve Pinetti, Senior Vice President of Sales & Marketing for Kimpton Hotels and Restaurants. Hotel Monaco is part of their premier collection. "Everything about Hotel Monaco appeals directly to the senses, and 'Guppy Love' offers one more unique way to relax, indulge and promote health of mind, body and spirit in our home-away-from-home atmosphere."[25]

The second part of our goldfish inspiration came from the peculiar growth of a goldfish. The average common goldfish is between three to four inches in length (ten centimeters), yet the largest in the world is almost six times that size! For comparison, imagine walking down the street and bumping into someone who's three stories tall.

How can there be such a disparity between regular goldfish and their monster cousins? Well, it turns out that the growth of the

---

25. https://purplegoldfish.com/its-always-5-oclock-kimpton/

goldfish is determined by five factors. Just like goldfish, not all businesses grow equally, and we believe that the growth of a product or service faces the same five factors that affect the growth of a goldfish.

#1. SIZE OF THE ENVIRONMENT = THE MARKET

GROWTH FACTOR: The size of the bowl or pond

IMPACT: Direct correlation. The larger the bowl or pond, the larger the goldfish can grow. Similarly, the smaller the market in business, the lesser the growth potential.

#2. NUMBER OF OTHER GOLDFISH IN THE BOWL OR POND = COMPETITION

GROWTH FACTOR: The number of goldfish in the same bowl or pond

IMPACT: Inverse correlation. The more goldfish, the less growth. Similarly, the less competition in business, the more growth opportunity exists.

#3. THE QUALITY OF THE WATER = THE ECONOMY

GROWTH FACTOR: The clarity and amount of nutrients in the water

IMPACT: Direct correlation. The better the quality, the larger the growth. Similarly, the weaker the economy or capital markets in business, the more difficult it is to grow.

FACT

A malnourished goldfish in a crowded, cloudy environment may only grow to two inches (five centimeters).

#4. THE FIRST 120 DAYS OF LIFE = STARTUP PHASE OR A NEW PRODUCT LAUNCH

GROWTH FACTOR: The nourishment and treatment received as a fry (baby goldfish)

IMPACT: Direct correlation. The lower the quality of the food, water, and treatment, the more the goldfish will be stunted for future growth. Similarly, in business, the stronger the leadership and capital for a start-up, the better the growth.

#5. GENETIC MAKEUP = DIFFERENTIATION

GROWTH FACTOR: The genetic makeup of the goldfish

IMPACT: Direct correlation. The poorer the genes or the less differentiated, the less the goldfish can grow. Similarly, in business, the more differentiated the product or service from the competition, the better the chance for growth.

FACT

The current *Guinness Book of World Records* holder for the largest goldfish hails from The Netherlands at a whopping 19 inches (50 centimeters). To put that in perspective, that's about the size of the average domestic cat.

WHICH OF THE FIVE FACTORS CAN YOU CONTROL?

Let's assume you have an existing product or service and have been in business for more than four months. Do you have any control over the market, your competition, or the economy? NO, NO, and NO.

The only thing you have control over is your business's genetic makeup or how you differentiate your product or service. In gold-fish terms, how do you stand out in a sea of sameness? We believe that differentiation can be driven through employee engagement.

Now, why the color green? The reasons for green are three-fold:

1. MARDI GRAS AND LAGNIAPPE – Lagniappe is creole for "a little something extra." Green is an ode to the birthplace of the word (New Orleans) and the colors of its most famous event (Mardi Gras).

The accepted story behind the original selection of the Mardi Gras colors originates from 1872 when the Grand Duke Alexis Romanoff of Russia visited New Orleans. It is said that the Grand Duke came to the city in pursuit of an actress named Lydia Thompson. During his stay, he was given the honor of selecting the official Mardi Gras colors by the Krewe of Rex. His selection of purple, green, and gold would also later become the colors of the House of Romanoff.

The 1892 Rex Parade theme first gave meaning to the official Mardi Gras colors. Inspired by New Orleans and the traditional colors, purple was symbolic of justice, green was symbolic of faith, and gold was symbolic of power.

2. BEYOND DOLLARS – Money is not a motivator. According to McKinsey,[26] numerous studies have shown that for people with

---

26. https://www.mckinsey.com/business-functions/organization/our-insights/motivating-people-getting-beyond-money

satisfactory salaries, non-financial motivators were more effective than extra cash in building long-term employee engagement in most sectors, job functions, and business contexts. Often financial rewards generate short-term boosts of energy that can have damaging, unintended consequences. When used poorly, monetary rewards can feel like coercion, an effect you see in the classic carrot-and-stick approach to motivation. According to leading research by Edward Deci, "Unless you're extremely careful with how you use rewards, you get people who are just working for the money. We need to compensate people fairly, but when we try to use money to motivate them to do tasks, it can very likely backfire on us."[27]

This becomes apparent when dealing with workers in an information economy. According to the Center for Talent Innovation (CTI), money is not the major motivator among college-educated workers. Today's employees are looking beyond conventional monetary rewards. And it doesn't take a huge budget. Many of these rewards can be free. Sylvia Ann Hewlett cites the results of a survey of remote workers where 83 percent of millennials and 75 percent of boomers say that the freedom to choose when and where they work motivates them to give 110 percent.[28]

3. GROWING - Green is about growth. When you are green, you are growing. When you are ripe, you begin to rot. Green is representative of the little things that can make the big difference in establishing culture.

TAKEAWAY

Look beyond dollars. Little things can make a big difference.

---

27. https://www.hrzone.com/community-voice/blogs/
    derekirvine/3-lessons-from-edward-deci-on-why-cash-is-not-king-for-employee
28. http://www.harvardbusiness.org/leadership-blogs/attract-and-keep-players-nonfinancial-rewards

CHAPTER 4

A LITTLE SOMETHING EXTRA

"We picked up one excellent word—a word worth traveling to New Orleans to get; a nice, limber, expressive, handy word—'lagniappe.'"

— Mark Twain from his autobiography
Life on the Mississippi

WHAT IF ...

What if there was a simple concept that could move the needle toward achieving differentiation, driving retention, reinforcing culture, and stimulating word of mouth? What if your execution was 100 percent targeted, with zero waste, and given with a personalized touch?

What is lagniappe? Lagniappe is a creole word meaning "the gift" or "to give more." The practice originated in Louisiana in the 1840s whereby a merchant would give a little something extra. It is a signature personal touch by the business that creates goodwill and promotes word of mouth.

According to Webster's:[29]

LAGNIAPPE (lan'yap, lăn-yăp') *Chiefly Southern Louisiana & Mississippi*

1. A small gift presented by a store owner to a customer with the customer's purchase.

2. An extra or unexpected gift or benefit. Also called regionally *boot.*

> Etymology: Creole < French "la" + Spanish "ñapa." Interesting fact: Napa comes from yapa, which means "additional gift" in the South American Indian language, Quechua, from the verb yapay "to give more."

ENTER SAMUEL LANGHORNE CLEMENS

According to Mark Twain in his autobiography *Life on the Mississippi*:[30]

---

29. https://www.merriam-webster.com/dictionary/lagniappe
30. https://www.amazon.com/Life-Mississippi-Twain-Original-Version-ebook/dp/B016032RTW

We picked up one excellent word—a word worth traveling to New Orleans to get; a nice limber, expressive, handy word—'lagniappe.' They pronounce it lanny-yap. It is Spanish—so they said. We discovered it at the head of a column of odds and ends in the [Times] Picayune [newspaper] the first day; heard twenty people use it the second; inquired what it meant the third; adopted it and got facility in swinging it the fourth. It has a restricted meaning, but I think the people spread it out a little when they choose. It is the equivalent of the thirteenth roll in a baker's dozen. It is something thrown in, gratis, for good measure. The custom originated in the Spanish quarter of the city. When a child or a servant buys something in a shop—or even the mayor or the governor, for aught I know—he finishes the operation by saying—'Give me something for lagniappe.' The shopman always responds; gives the child a bit of licorice-root, gives the servant a cheap cigar or a spool of thread, gives the governor—I don't know what he gives the governor; support, likely.

A Green Goldfish is any time a business purposely goes above and beyond to provide a little something extra. It's a marketing investment in your employees. It's that unexpected extra beyond compensation that is thrown in for good measure. Lagniappe helps drive differentiation, increases retention, promotes word of mouth, and reinforces corporate culture.

SO—IS IT JUST A BAKER'S DOZEN?

In order to understand a baker's dozen, we need to travel back to its origin in England. The concept dates back to the thirteenth century during the reign of Henry III. During this time, there was a perceived need for regulations controlling quality, pricing, and checking weights to avoid fraudulent activity. The Assize (Statute) of Bread and Ale[31] was instituted to regulate the price, weight, and quality of the bread and beer manufactured and sold in towns, villages, and hamlets.

Bakers who were found to have shortchanged customers could be liable for severe punishment such as losing a hand via an axe. To guard against the punishment, the baker would give 13 for the price of 12 to be certain of not being known as a cheat.

The irony is that the statute deals with weight and not the quantity. The merchants created the "baker's dozen" to change perception. They understood that one of the 13 could be lost, eaten, burnt, or ruined in some way, leaving the customer with the original legal dozen.

A baker's dozen has become expected. Nowadays when we walk into a bakery and buy a dozen bagels, we expect the thirteenth on the house. Therefore, it is not lagniappe. Now, if you provided a 14th bagel that would be an unexpected extra.

ACTS OF KINDNESS

Another way to think of employee lagniappe is as an act of kindness.

There are three types of acts of kindness:

- **Random Act of Kindness:** We've all seen this before. Good deeds or unexpected acts such as paying tolls, filling parking meters, or buying gas. They are usually one-off, feel-good activations. A random act of kindness draws upon gift economy principles. Engaging in giving without an expectation of immediate return.

---

31. https://en.wikipedia.org/wiki/Assize_of_Bread_and_Ale

- **Branded Act of Kindness:** This is the next level or kindness 2.0. Here the item given is usually tied closely with the brand and its positioning. It's less random, more planned, and potentially a series of activations. This has the feel of a traditional marketing campaign.

- **Lagniappe Act of Kindness:** At 3.0, kindness is imbedded into your brand. It is giving little unexpected extras (**G.L.U.E.**) as part of your DNA. This is rooted in the idea of "added value" to the transaction. Not a one off or a campaign, but an everyday practice that's focused on employees or customers. The beauty of creating Green and Purple Goldfish is that there is no waste when giving little extras to your current employees and customers. You are preaching to the choir—the folks who are already in church on Sunday. Folks you want to keep.

THE NEED FOR INNOVATION AND TROJAN MICE

Actions speak louder than words when it comes to employee experience and building a strong culture. Brands need to start taking small steps to add value to the experience over time. Here is a great analysis by Peter Fryar on the concept of Trojan Mice:[32]

> Much change is of the 'Trojan horse' variety. The planned changes are presented at a grand event (the Trojan Horse) amid much loud music, bright lights, and dry ice. More often than not, however, a few weeks later the organization will have settled back into its usual ways and rejected much of the change. This is usually because the change was too great to be properly understood and owned by the workforce. Trojan mice, on the other hand, are small, well-focused changes, which are introduced on an ongoing basis

32. https://jarche.com/2012/10/on-trojan-mice/

in an inconspicuous way. They are small enough to be understood and owned by all concerned, but their effects can be far-reaching. Collectively a few Trojan mice will change more than one Trojan horse ever could.

TAKEAWAY

Employers are finding that supporting and incentivizing their staff improves motivation and engagement, which in turn impacts productivity. Take care of employees first with an inside-out approach. Aim for increasing satisfaction and creating positive word of mouth. Your employees can become your best marketing asset.

CHAPTER 5

POWERED BY GIFT ECONOMY PRINCIPLES

"There are two types of economies. In a commodity (or exchange) economy, status is accorded to those who have the most. In a gift economy, status is accorded to those who give the most to others."

— Lewis Hyde

EXPLORING THE IDEAS OF SURPLUS AND STATUS

What is a gift economy and how does it relate to culture? According to Wikipedia, "In the social sciences, a gift economy (or gift culture) is a society where valuable goods and services are regularly given without any explicit agreement for immediate or future rewards. Ideally, simultaneous or recurring giving serves to circulate and redistribute valuables within the community."[33]

A gift economy is the opposite of a market economy. In a market economy there is an exact exchange of values (quid pro quo). It is our belief that a hybrid called the lagniappe economy can sit between the two. Daniel Pink, the author of several books including *Drive: The Surprising Truth About What Motivates Us,* speaks on the common thread between gift economy and employee engagement. Pink boils it down to just three factors: autonomy, mastery, and purpose. The "little something extra" for employees lies in these three gifts. Gift economy for corporate culture is about motivation and moving past the "carrot-or-the-stick" method that businesses have been using for years.

---

33. https://en.wikipedia.org/wiki/Gift_economy

Can marketing lagniappe live in the middle? Here is a great analysis from a post by Kevin von Duuglas-ittu on gift economies:

> This does not mean that the Gift Economy ... and the Market Economy of business are incompatible, not in the least. In fact, many if not most of our business exchanges are grounded in gift-based relationships whose "gift" nature we simply are unconscious of and just assume. If you develop a keen eye for the gift-giving environment and think about all the things that gift-giving in those environments signal, 1. A surplus others want to attach themselves to, 2. A magnanimous respect for the relationship beyond all else, 3. A debt structure that is positive, you will see that Gift Economy and Market Economy can exist in the same ecosystem.

Let's examine each of the three through the lens of a lagniappe economy:

1. **Surplus:** the idea of surplus is grounded in giving extra or creating an inequality as lagniappe means "something that is added." Lagniappe is the practice by the business of giving little unexpected extras.

2. **Respect**: The gift or little extra is about the respect for the relationship. It becomes a beacon, a sign that shows you care. It's a physical sign of goodwill and employee appreciation.

3. **Positive**: A debt structure is created that is positive. This speaks to exceeding expectations by giving extra. The idea of an equal exchange (market exchange) is a myth in marketing. You either exceed or fall short of expectations. Providing that extra value provides an inequality that is positive. The positive effect leads to a sort of indebtedness or need for reciprocity.

THE BENEFIT OF SURPLUS IS STATUS

As a business, why would you want to incorporate gift economy principles into your culture? We believe there are three distinct reasons and corresponding benefits of the status gained through marketing lagniappe:

1. **Positioning**: stand out from your competition. If everyone is providing x, the fact that you provide x + y (gift) differentiates your offering. **Benefit: Differentiation**

2. **Loyalty**: give the little extra (gift) to enhance employee experience. This creates a bond between the business and the employee. The benefit of that bond is increased loyalty as a form of repayment. **Benefit: Retention**

3. **Reciprocity**: give extra to create goodwill (inequality). That inequality is repaid by positive word of mouth. The best form of marketing is via positive word of mouth. By giving signature extras, you provide something for your employees to talk, tweet, blog, Glassdoor, or Facebook about. **Benefit: Referrals**

PART II:

THE FIVE INGREDIENTS OR R.U.L.E.S. OF A GREEN GOLDFISH

CHAPTER 6

RELEVANT

*"Take great care of your people, they'll take great
care of your customers, and your customers
will come back and back and back."*

— Bill Marriott Sr.

MAKING EMPLOYEE LAGNIAPPE IS LIKE MAKING JAMBALAYA

Have you ever made jambalaya? It's a bunch of different ingredients all thrown in together. The chef takes a look at what's lying around in the kitchen, throws it all into a pot, and then lets it stew with some spices thrown in and voila`! You have yourself jambalaya or a Green Goldfish.

Here are the five main ingredients of a Green Goldfish or, if you are an acronym fan (like we are), the R.U.L.E.S.:

Relevant: The item or benefit should be of value to your employees.

Unexpected: The extra benefit or gift should leverage the benefit of surprise. It is something thrown in for good measure.

Limited: If it's a small token or gift, try to select something that's rare, hard to find, or unique to your business.

Expressive: Many times, the lagniappe comes down to the gesture. It becomes more about "how" it is given, as opposed to what is given.

Sticky: Is it memorable enough that the employees will want to share their experience by telling one friend or a few hundred?

KEEPING IT RELEVANT

The first **R**.U.L.E.S. ingredient, and probably the most important, for a Green Goldfish is being **relevant.** If it's just a throw-in or SWAG (stuff we all get), it's probably not that relevant. A Green Goldfish needs to be something that is valued by your employees.

All the perks in the world won't make a difference if the overall culture doesn't include the most important factors. Among them: Do employees feel valued? Are there opportunities to grow? Do employees have good relationships with their managers?

Employers are finding that supporting and providing incentives for their staff improves motivation and engagement, which in turn impacts productivity.[34]

Let's look at a handful of relevant examples from Clif Bar:

- The Emeryville, California, based nutrition company offers employees a half-hour of paid time to work out. Additionally, employees get 2.5 hours of free personal training per year.

- Environmental issues are very important to the company. Clif Bar gives their employees $6,500 toward the purchase of a fuel-efficient vehicle and $1,000 to do an energy upgrade on their home.

- The company was born on a bike. Clif Bar will give an employee $500 for the purchase of a commuter bike so long as the employee agrees to commute by bike at least twice a month.

- Employees receive a $350 stipend to help cover the entry costs for races, events, and competitions.

- Every week the company assembles for a company breakfast—bagels, fresh fruit, eggs, oatmeal, juice, bacon, sausage, and more are served—and the team shares news, announcements, and a consumer's letter of the week.

---

34. https://www.chicagobusiness.com/article/20120331/ISSUE02/120329728/
chicago-s-best-places-to-work-2012-why-your-perks-aren-t-working

TAKEAWAY STAT

Clif Bar enjoys a retention rate of 96 percent.

CHAPTER 7

UNEXPECTED

"So what exactly is 'surprise and delight?'
It's when you give your customer something—that little
gift or 'extra mile'—that they didn't expect.
Surprise and delight is that small benevolent act that
shows that you put the customer first, and that
you're willing to make their experience special."

— Marc Schiller

WHAT THE HELL IS A SCHEMA?

Steve Knox wrote an article in *Ad Age* titled, "Why Effective Word of Mouth Disrupts Schemas."[35] The premise of the article is how you can leverage cognitive disruption to drive word of mouth. By doing something unexpected, you literally force people to talk about their experience.

First off let us admit we had no clue what a "schema" was. So here is our interpretation of the word. Our brain remains typically in a static state. It relies on developing cognitive schemas to figure out how the world works. It recognizes patterns and adapts behavior accordingly. It basically doesn't want to have to think. For example, every day you get into the car and you know instinctively to drive on the right side of the road. Fast forward and you're on a trip to the UK or Australia. The first time you drive on the left side, it throws you for a loop. It's disruptive to your normal driving schema so it forces the brain to think and thereby, it elicits discussion (i.e. word of mouth).

Steve provided some great examples in his article, including a new Secret deodorant from P&G. The deodorant utilizes moisture activated ingredients that kick in when you sweat. The brand understood that this could be positioned against the traditional schema of the more you work out, the more you sweat, and the worse you smell. The counter-intuitive tagline for the brand became, "The More You Move, the Better You Smell." Did it get people talking? A staggering 51,000 consumers posted comments on P&G's website about the product.

We started thinking how this idea of disruption applies to the concept of engagement and culture. The second ingredient in the R.U.L.E.S. is the concept of being **Unexpected**. It's that little something unexpected that triggers the disruption of our schemas.

---

35. http://customerthink.com/disrupt_schemas_via_surprise_and_delight/

Let's face it, most companies fail to deliver an exceptional employee experience. It's only when a brand goes above and beyond that we get shocked.

Brazilian manufacturer Semco has a whole school of unexpected Green Goldfish. Here are some examples:

- All employees, including union members, have full access to all financials. Access is one thing, understanding is another. To educate its employees, Semco has created cartoons to help explain the financial data.

- Semco offers Up and Down Pay. The company does its best to accommodate employees who are going through a phase where they'd rather work less and lower their pay accordingly.

- Employees at Semco dictate their own salary. Twice a year they are given the chance to set their compensation structure.

- Semco's employees have the flexibility to set their own hours.

- Semco believes that it is important to meet people interested in working with their company, even if this interest is not immediate or there are no current opportunities. This led them to create the program they call Date Semco. It's good for prospective employees and current ones so each gets a chance to meet in order to determine if the fit is right.

- Employees are not allowed to sit in the same place two days in a row. This encourages collaboration and eliminates the need for managers to track time spent by employees at their desk.

CHAPTER 8

LIMITED

*"America has believed that in differentiation, not in uni-
formity, lies the path of progress. It acted on this belief;
it has advanced human happiness, and it has prospered."*

— Louis Brandeis

SIGNATURE TOUCH

The third of the R.U.L.E.S. is the concept of being **limited**. What does limited mean? If it's a small token or extra, it means selecting something unique to your business. Ideally, you want it to be signature to your brand. It is something rare, different, or just plain hard to find elsewhere. A limited extra helps you differentiate yourself in the marketplace, while providing insurance against being copied by competitors.

Assurance, a Schaumburg, Illinois, based insurance brokerage, has a whole host of incentives for its employees, including Starbucks coffee, yoga classes, and a Wii station plus big-ticket items such as referral bonuses for new clients, education reimbursements, and companywide bonuses for reaching goals. Yet the benefits with the biggest impact on culture seem to be those that bring employees together. "I think we're really thoughtful about the things we emphasize," says Jackie Gould, the company's chief operating officer. "A lot of [the benefits] aren't really about the money. It's more about fostering the relationships."[36]

According to Steven Handmaker, CMO at Assurance, culture is the secret sauce.[37] Each year the company rallies around a theme and an accompanying song. The songs are typically from the 1980s with a fun/irreverent feel. In 2017, it was the "Power of Love" by Huey Lewis. The previous year was Salt-N-Pepa's "Push It," and the theme was wellness. Their Shared Success bonus program is based on four components, two of which are financial and two that tie in with the cultural theme. For example, during the wellness year, everyone in the company would achieve success if 84 percent of the company completed a 5K race at some point during the year. Over 95 percent ended up completing a race. In 2017, the metric

36. https://www.chicagobusiness.com/article/20120331/ISSUE02/120329728/
   chicago-s-best-places-to-work-2012-why-your-perks-aren-t-working
37. https://www.assuranceagency.com/about-us/a-team/steven-handmaker

was handwritten notes. Twenty were meant for customers and 17 for friends/family. Over the last few years, Assurance has become a fixture on Fortune's Best Place to Work (for Small to Medium businesses), and they won "Best Place to Work in Chicago" by the Chicago Tribune.[38] Not bad for a "boring" insurance brokerage.

TAKEAWAY

Engage employees and fire their imaginations. Set your values and trust your employees to make the right decisions. A transformation from the ground up is more sustainable than from the top down.

---

38. http://www.chicagotribune.com/business/careers/topworkplaces/ct-top-workplaces-2016-midsize-assurance-1111-biz-20161111-story.html

CHAPTER 9

EXPRESSIVE

"If you treat employees as if they make a difference to the company, they will make a difference to the company."

— Dr. James Goodnight, co-founder of SAS Institute

THE IMPORTANCE OF HOW

The fourth of the R.U.L.E.S. is about being **expressive**. Expressive speaks to "how you give" as opposed to "what you give." A Green Goldfish is a beacon. It's a sign that shows you care. Little extras and touches that demonstrate that your team members matter.

Nurse Next Door is a Canadian home healthcare provider. The company first showed up in Purple Goldfish Project. They had an interesting way of handling mistakes with customers. And let's face it, we all make mistakes. It's how you handle them that makes the difference. In addition to sending a handwritten note, Nurse Next Door also sends a freshly baked apple pie to apologize. Literally, a humble pie.

Nurse Next Door has two unique Green Goldfish. The first is the Flowerbucks program. As a core value-driven organization, team members demonstrating core values earn an in-house currency called "Flowerbucks." Each quarter the company holds Flowerbuck Auctions to celebrate core value award winners and auction off prizes ranging from gift cards to iPads and even trips.

The second program involves focusing employees on their personal dreams. Nurse Next Door sits down with employees to uncover their goals. They've been able to support all sorts of dreams ranging from learning to sail to learning a new language to buying a home to travelling.

Both of these programs converged recently to make one really cool story. At a Flowerbuck Auction, one of their employees ended up winning a trip because her co-workers gave her their flowerbucks. They did this because they learned her dream was to travel to South America and volunteer to teach English. All she needed was the airline ticket, so her coworkers donated their own flowerbucks.[39] A great example of Paying It Forward.

---

39. https://www.youtube.com/watch?v=QWKthxnNCWk#action=share

CHAPTER 10

STICKY

"Why wait to be memorable?"

— Tony Robbins

STICKING OUT IN A SEA OF SAMENESS

The fifth of the R.U.L.E.S. is **sticky**. You want something that sticks. A strong extra that promotes word of mouth. Your Green Goldfish needs to be memorable and talkable. Two questions to ask yourself: 1. Is it water cooler material? 2. Will your employees want to tell three people or 3,000?

Let's look at a sticky example from Peppercomm:

About six years ago, Steve Cody, one of Peppercomm's founders and a managing partner, started taking stand-up comedy classes for fun. He worked with Clayton Fletcher, a touring stand-up comedian, to build his chops.

"As he started doing more and more stand-up, he started to recognize that although he was very good at client meetings and presentations, he was getting a lot better," says Deborah Brown, Partner and Managing Director, Strategic Development.[40] Brown credits the training with developing not only speaking skills but listening skills as well. It wasn't long before the entire management committee at Peppercomm was taking comedy training. It was sprung on the team at an offsite meeting. Soon after that, everyone in the company was involved. "For the past five years, it's become part of our DNA," Brown says.

In fact, comedy training is now mandatory at the agency and is part of the onboarding process. The training consists of learning about different types of comedy such as observational humor. It's become a great way to meet the new hires with "graduation" consisting of a five-minute set of stand-up. The agency has created fundraisers out of the performances and has even incorporated them into agency offsite meetings.

---

40. http://www.peppercomm.com/why-stand-up-comedy-is-good-for-your-business/

The training has become an integral part of Peppercomm. Deborah Brown credits it with improving productivity, building teamwork, and injecting fun into the agency. Humor is now part of the fabric of Peppercomm, whether it takes the form of spicing up an interoffice email or creating a funny video for a client pitch. The agency has received a number of positive stories in the press and has recently started to extend the training to existing and prospective clients.

GETTING THE LAST LAUGH

The biggest benefactor has been the culture at Peppercomm. The agency was recognized by Crain's as one of the Top 50 places to work in New York City. In case you are interested, here are the top five in descending order:

> 5. Microsoft
>
> 4. Conductor
>
> 3. Allison + Partners
>
> 2. Squarespace
>
> Drumroll please ... 1. Peppercomm

This whole approach of taking business but not yourself seriously can be summed up in one quote from Deborah Brown:

> Comedy training does more than create a unique culture. It produces a better business executive, someone who is just a tad ahead of their peers when it comes to listening skills, building audience rapport, and thinking in a nanosecond. Happy, funny employees are also the reason why we maintain so many long-term client

relationships, experience low turnover, and produce amazing creativity. And that's no joke.[41]

Now, let's look at the 15 different types of Green Goldfish.

---

41. https://purplegoldfish.com/employee-engagement-is-a-laughing-matter-peppercom/

PART III:

15 TYPES OF GREEN GOLDFISH

CHAPTER 11

BUILDING, BELONGING, AND BECOMING

"There are no traffic jams along the extra mile."

— Roger Staubach

WHERE IS THE LOVE?

Motivation for employees is sagging. Recent reports show that motivation has fallen off at more than half of all companies. In difficult economic times, how can companies boost employee morale and drive high performance? The simple answer is doing the little extras beyond compensation to demonstrate commitment to your employees. The Green Goldfish Project on List.ly[42] has taken a look at how companies go above and beyond to create signature extras. In examining the 1,001 examples of employee lagniappe, a few key themes emerged. Specifically, the different types of Green Goldfish can be categorized as the Three **B**'s:

1. **B**uilding: Creating a stable environment where people can thrive

2. **B**elonging: Enabling high functioning teams and recognizing their efforts

3. **B**ecoming: Empowering employees to learn, give back, and take control of their destiny

CARING AND DOING THE RIGHT THING

Google sets the gold standard for taking care of its employees. No stone is left unturned in their quest to provide a welcoming and happy work environment. WHY? Here's an answer according to Google's Chief People Officer Laszlo Bock. He says, "It turns out that the reason we're doing these things for employees is not because it's important to the business, but simply because it's the right thing to do. When it comes down to it, it's better to work for a company who cares about you than a company who doesn't. And

---

42. https://list.ly/list/1OE-green-goldfish-project?feature=search

from a company standpoint, that makes it better to care than not to care."[43]

But there may be a more important reason according to Shawn Achor, CEO and founder of Good Think. He says, "These aren't just PR Gimmicks. Smart companies cultivate these kinds of working environments. Because every time an employee experiences a small burst of happiness, they get primed for creativity and innovation. They see solutions they might otherwise have missed."[44]

Google holds the top spot in the Green Goldfish Project with 20 entries. Let's have a look at a bakers dozen of their examples.

BUILDING: ONBOARDING AND FOOD & BEVERAGE

Breakfast, lunch, dinner, and the Google 15 comprise one of the most often cited perks of working at Google: the food. Google feeds its employees well. If you work at the Googleplex, you can eat breakfast, lunch, and dinner free of charge. There are several cafés located throughout the campus, and employees can eat at any of them. The main café is Charlie's Place. The café takes its name from Google's first lead chef, Charlie Ayers. Before creating meals for Googlers, Ayers was the chef for the Grateful Dead. Although Ayers left Google in 2005, the café still bears his name. The café has several stations, each offering different kinds of cuisine. Options range from vegetarian dishes to sushi to ethnic foods from around the world. Google's culture promotes the use of fresh organic foods and healthy meals. But when everything is free and you can eat whenever you want, it's easy to go overboard. That's where the Google 15 comes in. It refers to the 15 pounds many new Google employees put on once they start taking advantage of all the meals and snacks. Other cafés at the Googleplex include the Pacific Café, Charleston Café, Café 150, and the appropriately named No Name

---

43. https://purplegoldfish.com/learning-green-goldfish-google-15-ways-drive-employee-engagement/
44. http://goodthinkinc.com/success-magazine-you-have-to-see-your-happiness-to-believe-it/

Café. Each offers employees several choices for every meal. Google serves up more than 200 recipes in these cafés every day.[45]

BUILDING: SHELTER AND WELLNESS

The Lamborghini of toilets is a definite Green Goldfish. Googlers have access to some of the most high-tech toilets around. These Japanese johns offer washing and drying of your nether regions as well as the mysterious "wand cleaning." Both the wash water and the seat itself can be warmed or cooled depending on your preference.[46]

One perk about working at Google is that Gawker never posts a photo of you swimming in one of the Googleplex's lap pools. The outdoor mini-pools are like water treadmills: a strong current allows employees to swim and swim and go nowhere. Luckily, according to *How Stuff Works*, lifeguards are always on duty in case someone gets in over their head.[47]

BUILDING: TIME AWAY AND THE MODERN FAMILY

Google is giving its employees in same-sex relationships extra cash to cover their partners' health benefits. Currently, when receiving partner health care coverage, same-sex domestic partners are subject to an extra tax that straight, married couples aren't required to pay. Google is taking the burden of paying this tax on itself by compensating partnered LGBT employees for the amount of the tax, which comes to a bit more than $1,000 each year. This benefit will also cover any dependents of the partner in the same-sex couple.[48]

---

45. https://computer.howstuffworks.com/googleplex1.htm
46. https://www.huffingtonpost.com/2012/01/30/google-benefits-employee-perks_n_1242707. html#s649145&title=Japanese_Toto_Toilets
47. https://www.huffingtonpost.com/2012/01/30/google-benefits-employee-perks_n_1242707. html#s649180&title=Endless_Lap_Pools
48. https://mashable.com/2010/07/01/google-lgbt-health/

BELONGING: RETIREMENT AND FLEXIBILITY

Taken from a post by Meghan Casserly in *Forbes*, "In a rare interview with Chief People Officer Laszlo Bock I discovered that the latest perk for Googlers extends into the afterlife. 'This might sound ridiculous,' Bock told me recently in a conversation on the ever-evolving benefits at Google, 'But we've announced death benefits at Google.' Should a U.S. Googler pass away while under the employ of the search giant, their surviving spouse or domestic partner will receive a check for 50 percent of the employee's salary every year for the next decade. Even more surprising, a Google spokesperson confirms that there's 'no tenure requirement' for this benefit, meaning most Google employees qualify."[49]

Former Google Executive Marissa Mayer believes women are especially susceptible to burning out because they are faced with more demands in the home. "What causes burnout, Mayer believes, is not working too hard," Hanna Rosin writes in her interview with Mayer in the book, *The End of Men: The Rise of Women.*[50] People, she [Mayer] believes, "...can work arbitrarily hard for an arbitrary amount of time, but they will become resentful if work makes them miss things that are really important to them." Mayer provided a story for how she kept one Google executive, whom she calls Katy, from quitting in the book,

> Katy loved her job and she loved her team and she didn't mind staying late to help out. What was bothering Katy was something entirely different. Often, Katy confessed, she showed up late at her children's events because a meeting went overly long for no important reason other than meetings tend to go long. And she hated having her children watch her walk in late. For Mayer, this was a no-brainer. She instituted

49. https://www.huffingtonpost.com/2012/01/30/google-benefits-employee-perks_n_1242707.html
50. https://www.amazon.com/End-Men-Rise-Women/dp/1594488045

a Katy-tailored rule. If Katy had told her earlier that she had to leave at four to get to a soccer game, then Mayer would make sure Katy could leave at four. Even if there was only five minutes left to a meeting, even if Google co-founder Sergey Brin himself was mid-sentence and expecting an answer from Katy, Mayer would say 'Katy's gotta go' and Katy would walk out the door and answer the questions later by e-mail after the kids were in bed.

TAKEAWAY

The key to sustaining loyalty in employees is making sure they get to do the things that are most important to them outside of work.

BELONGING: TEAM BUILDING AND TRANSPARENCY

Google knows how to roll. It has a bowling alley for employees.

Google's Conference Bike is used as a team-building exercise for new employees. It has four wheels and five riders who work together to move it around.[51]

"TGIF" meetings are one of the things shaping culture at the search leader. They tend to happen most Fridays according to Craig Silverstein, who joined the founders as Google's first employee in 1998. TGIF, where any Googler is free to ask the founders any company-related question, has become a fixture of the culture.[52]

---

51. http://www.pcmag.com/slideshow_viewer/0,3253,l=238614&a=238614&po=1,00.asp

52. https://logosconsulting.net/wp-content/uploads/2016/02/Jocelyn-Jaixin-Cao-Capstone-Developing-the-Why-Frame.pdf

BELONGING: ATTABOYS AND ATTAGIRLS

The Founders' Award, Google's most significant and high-profile recognition program, is designed to give extraordinary rewards for extraordinary team accomplishments. While there's no single yardstick for measuring achievement, a general rule of thumb is that the team being rewarded has accomplished something that created tremendous value for Google. The awards pay out in the form of Google Stock Units that vest over time. Team members receive awards based on their level of involvement and contribution, and the largest awards to individuals can reach several million dollars. In 2005, Google awarded approximately $45 million in restricted stock to employees working on 11 different projects.[53]

BECOMING: TRAINING AND DEVELOPMENT

Google's "CareerGuru" program matches Google executives with Google employees to provide confidential, one-on-one career coaching and guidance around the subjects of work-life balance, personal and professional development, communication styles, and conflict resolution, among others.[54]

BECOMING: GIVING BACK AND PAYING IT FORWARD

As a part of Google Outreach, Google teams up with charitable organizations and NGOs to leverage Google Earth to promote their causes.

53. https://www.amazon.com/gp/search?index=books&linkCode=qs&keywords=9789814365062
54. http://www.businessinsider.com/the-25-best-places-to-work-around-the-world-2012-11

BECOMING: EMPOWERING DREAMS AND GOALS

According to Jonathan Strickland in an article[55] titled "How the Googleplex Works," the company allows its employees to use up to 20 percent of their week at Google to pursue special projects. That means for every standard workweek, employees can take a full day to work on a project unrelated to their normal workload. Many of Google's products (i.e. Gmail and Google News) started out as pet projects in the 20 percent time program.

---

55. https://computer.howstuffworks.com/googleplex.htm

CHAPTER 12

BUILDING: RECRUITING AND ONBOARDING

*"We don't know where our first impressions
come from or precisely what they mean,
so, we don't always appreciate their fragility."*

— Malcolm Gladwell, Author of *The Tipping Point*

FIRST IMPRESSIONS

Attitudes begin to form at the initial point of contact with an organization. There is no better place to start applying G.L.U.E. than when you are recruiting and eventually welcoming new employees to your company. Smart companies take advantage of these early days in order to ensure a strong, productive, and dedicated workforce. "The way you manage the transition of somebody into your culture speaks volumes about the culture to the person coming in, because you're making those first early impressions and they know what's expected of them," says George Bradt, Managing Director at PrimeGenesis.[56]

ONBOARDING

The formal transition process for new employees is called onboarding. Here's how it is defined:

> Onboarding, also known as organizational socialization, refers to the mechanism through which new employees acquire the necessary knowledge, skills, and behaviors to become effective organizational members and insiders. Tactics used in this process include formal meetings, lectures, videos, printed materials, or computer-based orientations to introduce newcomers to their new jobs and organizations.[57]

Unfortunately, less than 25 percent of organizations have a formal onboarding process. According to onboarding pioneer and expert George Bradt, "Most organizations haven't thought things through in advance. On their first day, they are welcomed by such confidence-building remarks as: Oh, you're here. We'd better find you an office."

---

56. https://www.inc.com/winning-workplaces/articles/201105/employee-onboarding-done-better.html
57. https://en.wikipedia.org/wiki/Onboarding

WHY IS ONBOARDING CRITICAL?

Research shows that employees make the critical decision to stay or leave within the first six months. When new hires participate in an onboarding program, the company can "maximize retention, engagement, and productivity."[58] Socialization efforts lead to positive outcomes for new employees, including higher job satisfaction, better job performance, greater organizational commitment, and reduction in stress.

Yet, culturally onboarding new hires can be a real challenge. While sleek videos, laminated pocket cards, and lobby placards may help employees memorize the company values, the actual understanding of how to "live" the company values can be a whole other story. Your culture is only as cohesive as the people willing to live out the shared values. Once again, actions speak louder than words.

Having a diverse range of ways to welcome a new hire is critical to establishing a healthy employer-employee relationship.

Here is a baker's dozen of companies that purposefully go the extra mile to engage new team members.

WELCOME WAGON

The J. M. Smucker Company sends new hires a gift basket to their homes.[59]

Intel's new hires have dedicated greeters and gifts waiting for them when they arrive on their first days as a part of their hands-on new employee orientation.[60]

---

58. https://www.scribd.com/document/260057030/Onboarding-Toolkit-for-HR-Professionals

59. https://www.businessinsider.com/companies-with-awesome-perks-2012-10

60. https://www.businessinsider.com/the-25-best-places-to-work-around-the-world-2012-11

Online glasses manufacturer **Warby Parker** gives a welcome package to new employees. The package includes the founders' favorite pretzels and a gift certificate to a Thai restaurant since the founders lived off Thai food during their startup phase.

BUDDIES AND CUSTOMIZATION

Workspaces can be personalized. **Asana** gives each employee $10,000 to spend on their office setup. The most common choice is a sweet motorized desk that allows a person to sit or stand just by hitting a button (because we all know stand-up desks can save your life). The workspace customization is just one step in the onboarding process at Asana. The company outlines five steps in a recent post. They are summarized here:

1. **Minimize Chores:** Asana sets up their desk and computer in advance and provides $10K for further customization.

2. **Assign a Buddy:** A co-worker with tenure gets assigned to the new developer.

3. **Add Value on Day One**: New employees must ship something on Day One. It could be a tiny product improvement or a fix to a bug or a typo—anything.

4. **Meet the Team:** The buddy schedules a series of learning sessions on various engineering topics over the first few weeks.

5. **Starter Project:** Each new hire gets the same starter project—build a small chat application.

Capital One runs a Buddy Assimilation Program. The program matches veterans with newcomers. "Buddies" show the newbies around, have lunch with them, and act as a resource. After a month of training, new employees work "in the nest" for two weeks fielding incoming calls with plenty of support. Hands go up whenever a trainee has a question, and a roving supervisor runs over to help. Once on their own, employees work within teams. But they're never far from a helping hand as team leaders and "floor walkers" decked in bright red and yellow vests are always available to answer questions.[61]

At the social media master company, **Twitter,** all new hire desks are strategically placed next to the vital team member that they will be working with most from day one. Not to mention that each new employee is greeted with a T-shirt, a bottle of wine, and a customized email address. To add to the fun of the first day jitters, Twitter's CEO eats breakfast with all new hires, takes them on a tour of the company space, and ends the day with group program training specific to each person's new role.[62]

Every associate at **W. L. Gore & Associates** has a sponsor who coaches, mentors, and commits to helping that person succeed at the company.[63]

UNDERSTANDING THE BUSINESS

USAA figuratively runs a Boot Camp. The insurance provider for military members and their families has an interesting onboarding process for new employees. Training includes trying on military fatigues, eating MREs (ready to eat meals), and reading letters from family members.[64]

61. https://www.tampabay.com/news/business/workinglife/
    capital-ones-open-culture-helps-make-it-one-of-tampa-bays-top-workplaces/1227026
62. https://www.saplinghr.com/blog/top-7-employee-onboarding-programs
63. https://www.businessinsider.com/the-25-best-places-to-work-around-the-world-2012-11
64. https://purplegoldfish.com/12-effective-ways-to-increase-employee-engagement/

Exposure makes a difference in performance. According to *Fast Company*,[65] that's the finding of Adam Grant, a Wharton professor who studied the training given to 71 new call center employees of a mid-western software firm. According to the study, one group of trainees was chosen to meet an 'internal customer'—an employee of another department whose salary depends on the sales that the new hires make—during their initial training. In combination with some inspirational words from the CEO, this contact with a real live beneficiary significantly improved both sales and revenue during the employees' first seven weeks. The difference? A not-insignificant 20 percent improvement in revenue per shift. Leadership messages from the CEO about purpose, vision, mission, and meaning, however, had no such effect on their own.

WRITING THE SHIP

According to Harvard Professor and noted author Teresa Amabile, the ability to track small wins can help motivate big accomplishments. Rituals like writing in a diary can be a strong influencer. The number one driver for inner work-life is making progress on meaningful work. Reflection can become an important part of the process.

New hires at custom t-shirt company **CustomInk** receive a blank journal. They are encouraged to record any interesting things they learn about the company in their notebook during their orientation or any questions they would like to ask. New hires are also asked to record instances where they've seen CustomInk's values in action. At the 30-day mark, new hires convene to share what they've noted in their journals. Making new hires accountable for noticing

---

65. https://www.fastcompany.com/3004701/want-motivated-employees-put-them-contact-people-they-help

how their colleagues and managers live those values every day helps brings those behaviors to life.[66]

PICTURE THIS

Hulu has an interesting approach to reinforce culture. The company encourages employees [Hulugans] to bring their passions to work and has an interesting way of incorporating them during the onboarding process. In the words of John Foster, Hulu's Head of Talent and Organization, "When you enter our office, the first thing you notice is a wall of portraits with every team member showing off a bit of his or her personality. From this gigantic photo wall, even a casual visitor will quickly notice that our people are our most precious asset." Hulu hires a professional photographer to shoot all new hires. The only direction by Hulu is to bring whatever you are passionate about. The pictures are then placed in the lobby for all to see. Hundreds of portraits adorn the wall.

GAMIFY

New employees at **Snagajob** are asked to share their unique talents and experiences in a brief questionnaire. The answers are shared among employees over the company's employee-only online network. When new hires [Snaggers] are introduced at weekly company-wide meetings, employees are quizzed about the responses and get token rewards such as candy for each correct answer. "It's a fun way to hold our employees accountable for learning about our new Snaggers," says Betsy Kersey, whose title at Snagajob is Director of People.[67]

---

66. https://www.scribd.com/document/113370730/Top-Ten-People-Practices-from-the-2012-Best-Small-Medium-Workplaces-List

67. https://www.entrepreneur.com/article/220512

For the newbies at **L'Oréal**, the Fit Culture App is available in 11 different languages. As an added bonus to their six-month onboarding program, L'Oréal provides videos, testimonials, quizzes, and games through the app as a way to "give each and every employee … the keys to succeed in full alignment with company values such as multiculturalism, diversity, and inclusion," says Laurent Reich, Director of International Learning Practice. By the way, this is the first app that was developed and custom-made by a company to introduce and assist new hires in learning the company culture.[68]

RETURNSHIPS

TD Bank worked with the University of Toronto's Rotman School of Management to develop the Rotman Back to Work program for women who have been out of the workforce for over eight years. They also operate the in-house "Back to Business" rotational work program for women returning to work.

CHECK-INS

When employees join **Davies PR**, they are given a 3-month, 6-month, 9-month, and 12-month review to ensure they get a "Best Start" at Davies. After one year at the company, employees receive annual 360-degree reviews where they are assessed by their co-workers.

TECHNOLOGY SPURRING DIALOGUE

Companies are using new tools and procedures to assimilate their latest hires. **Veson Nautical**, a Boston-based software developer for risk management for the maritime industry, instituted a new program called FastStart, an online tool from consulting firm Bless-

---

68. https://www.loreal.com/media/press-releases/2017/june/fit-app-launches

ing White that aligns work styles and priorities between new employees and managers. "The manager ranks the skills important and less important to the job, and the employee does the same," says Sarah Taffee, director of human resources and organization effectiveness at Veson Nautical. "The employee has the opportunity to compare their own answers with their manager's answers, and then the system guides them through how to have an open discussion about those things."[69]

FINDING YOUR WAY & LOST IN SPACE

Box.net gives entry level employees three months to explore all the different departments of the company, and they train them so that they know their products and services backward and forward—and then they allow the employee to choose what department they feel is the best fit for them.[70]

There is one program at Brazilian manufacturer **Semco** that allows people to act like entrepreneurs at the company. Called Lost in Space, it assumes that young MBA recruits don't know what they want to do with their lives. According to CEO Ricardo Semler, "The program lets them roam the company for a year. They do what they want to do, move when they want to move, go where their interests take them; work for one, two, or six different units. At the end of the year, anyone they've worked for can offer them a job, or they can seek an opening in an area that interests them. If neither happens, we thank them for the year."[71]

---

69. https://www.inc.com/winning-workplaces/articles/201105/employee-onboarding-done-better.html
70. https://www.inc.com/winning-workplaces/articles/201105/employee-onboarding-done-better.html
71. https://www.amazon.com/Seven-Day-Weekend-Changing-Work-Works/dp/1591840260

PUTTING CULTURE ON THE FIRING LINE

A special offer is part of the four-week new hire paid training at **Zappos**. The training immerses the group into the culture and Zappos' laser focus on customer service. At the conclusion of training, everyone is offered a packet of cash to leave. The amount has been raised numerous times over the years, but the current offer is $3,000.

According to *Fast Company* co-founder Bill Taylor in *Harvard Business Review*, "It's a small practice with big implications: Companies don't engage emotionally with their customers—people do. If you want to create a memorable company, you have to fill your company with memorable people. How are you making sure that you're filling your organization with the right people? And how much are you willing to pay to find out?"[72]

Zappos challenges employees to fully commit to the company. Are you making a bold statement to reinforce your corporate culture? In case you're keeping score at home, roughly two to three percent of trainees at Zappos have taken the offer since it was rolled out.

---

72. https://hbr.org/video/2226602169001/why-zappos-pays-new-employees-to-quitand-you-should-too

MILLENNIAL MOMENT

According to a Deloitte Millennial Survey, six in 10 millennials agree that a "sense of purpose" is part of the reason they chose a new job. Ironically, the same survey states that roughly 75 percent of millennials believe that businesses are focused on their own agendas as opposed to making a greater impact on society. How can a company fill the gap in the disparity between what this generation believes *about* business and what they need *from* the business? Onboard your millennial employees by showcasing the company's direct societal impact. This generation craves being a part of something bigger than themselves. Make sure on day one your new hires make the connection. Play a video that highlights problems your organization has solved for real people. Have each team member share their contributing role and tasks. Share the information about local nonprofits that your company supports. Create genuine touch points within the first few weeks and months that ensure your new employees can visibly see the difference they are making for the greater good.[73]

Millennial Myth: This generation is self-absorbed, self-obsessed, and millennials are not team players.

Millennial Myth—Busted: A PayScale study revealed that 88 percent of millennials prefer a collaborative work environment than one driven by competition. This generation has been thrown into team settings since they were in grade school. They grew up in the

---

73. https://www2.deloitte.com/sg/en/pages/about-deloitte/articles/deloitte-millennial-survey-2015.html

age of inclusion, equality, and globalization, and therefore feel most comfortable in group and team settings. Onboarding should be no different. Make the effort to include the whole team during the process. The Generation Yers are much more likely to stick around for longer when you appeal to what's important to them.

CHAPTER 13

BUILDING: FOOD AND BEVERAGE

"When employees go home to their working-class neighborhoods, they compare jobs. One of our employees might say, 'I get a free, hot meal every day,' and his neighbor says, 'Really? I have to brown-bag it.' That is what I think of as WOMP – word-of-mouth potential – and it works as well in hiring as it does in marketing."

— Mike Jannini, Former Senior Executive, Marriott

REACHING THE HEART VIA THE STOMACH

L ittle things can make a big difference. Even silly little things like M&M's. "Food and beverage" is part of Building, the first step toward improving employee engagement. For a shining example, we head to the world's largest privately held software company.

Recognizing employees for their value to the company was part of the early SAS Institute heritage. People who worked for the company during its earliest days on Hillsborough Street (across from North Carolina State University) tell stories of piling into Dr. Jim Goodnight's station wagon and going down the street for pizza. SAS would pick up the tab whenever the company added another 100 customer sites to their list. A flexible work environment and some of the trademarks or beacons of the employee-friendly SAS culture, including M&M's and breakfast goodies, were born in the first months of the company's existence.[74]

HOUSTON, WE HAVE A PROBLEM

The culture of SAS Institute was formed out of direct experiences of its co-founder, Dr. James Goodnight. According to a case study by The Wharton School:

> Before founding SAS Institute, Goodnight worked briefly at NASA. What he found there was an environment in which people did not communicate. Any effort to build trust was absent: NASA used timecards to make sure that employees worked their full allotment of hours, and there were metal detectors to ensure that employees weren't stealing. That wasn't all. At NASA, executives were supposed to be seen as

---

74. https://www.sas.com/en_us/company-information/profile.html

'different' from the rest of the workers. There were special executive parking areas. Executives had their own break and dining area, with free, 'good' coffee. Everyone else had to dump a quarter into a vending machine if they wanted coffee or a soft drink. Goodnight decided that when he started his own company, he would create a very different environment.

From the outset, Goodnight worked toward creating a fun place to work with the work itself being the biggest reward, an environment that would harness creativity, providing all of the resources employees would need. The concept was simply living by the golden rule and treating people the way he would like to be treated. The entire approach can be summed up by an employee's quote in *Fast Company*, "You're given the freedom, the flexibility, and the resources to do your job. Because you're treated well, you treat the company well."[75]

GOOD BUSINESS

At a time when annual turnover in some information technology shops is as high as 30 percent and filling empty positions can cost anywhere from two to five times an employee's salary, IT firms are discovering what SAS Institute has known for decades: that it takes more than just a paycheck to keep their people happy. In SAS Institute's view, money should not be the key motivator. People who care primarily about the money can easily be bought. It's simple according to Dr. Goodnight. He says, "You have two choices. You can spend money on employees or headhunters and training, and it's about the same amount of money. So why not spend it on the employees?"

75. https://www.fastcompany.com/36173/sanity-inc

Is it working? SAS Institute has never had a single layoff in its entire history. It has less than 3 percent mean turnover, year over year growth, and a focus on long-term growth rather than satisfying shareholders' immediate requirements.

TAKEAWAY FACT

SAS averages 4,000 resumes for every job opening.

FREE FOR ALL

All of the benefits and perks are available to all employees, and everyone on campus is a SAS Institute employee: software engineers, salespeople, childcare workers, groundskeepers, and so on. Founder Goodnight believes strongly that people are much more committed if they are part of the company. All employees have the same exact bonus plan potential.

Here are some of the Good Eats examples at SAS Institute:

- Free fresh fruit every Monday, M&Ms on Wednesday, and breakfast goodies every Friday.

- Break rooms stocked with complimentary soft drinks, juices, crackers, coffee, and tea.

- Employee events and celebrations, including the annual Family Picnic, the elegant Winter Party, and end-of-the-month parties.

- Coffee with Goodnight. Once a month, employees can sign up to sit down with Dr. Goodnight for coffee and biscuits. (Goodnight has a supposed weakness for Biscuitville.) Eight to 10 employees get randomly selected for the hour-long session.

The first 15 minutes are an update on the state of the company by Goodnight with the remainder open for employee questions. No topics are off limits.

- Elmer Gibson plays piano at lunch in one of the SAS campus cafeterias three days a week. Meals are relatively cheap, and an emphasis is put on healthy food for employees.

- Sushi chef Namjoon Kim is one of three chefs who prepare made to order sushi rolls at lunch in the newest SAS employee cafeteria.

Let's look at a baker's dozen of companies that provide signature food and beverage extras.

FBNA is an acronym for "Free Beer, No A--holes." It is the pseudo tagline for marketing agency **Ryan Partnership** and an unofficial mantra for many others. Some like the Australian software company **Atlassian** make it a hiring requirement. The company has a recipe for selecting potential hires called the "beer test" according to co-founder Mike Cannon-Brookes. He says, "I ask myself, Would I find it interesting to have a beer with this job applicant?"

Here's a six-pack of beer and wine examples.

BEER O'CLOCK

At **Cirrus Logic**, weekly happy hours encourage engineers to interact and share ideas. The company also sponsors guitar lessons, on-site yoga, and photography courses. Every month, the company hosts "Cirrus Logic Rocks!"—a live music event featuring local musicians—on its outdoor patio.[76]

---

76. http://fortune.com/2012/10/25/the-25-best-medium-size-companies-to-work-for/

It's the tasty perk everyone wants but few companies provide: Free Beer. Cold brew is always on tap at **HubSpot's** headquarters in Cambridge, Massachusetts, where the kitchen has a designated beer fridge stocked with at least 50 different brands. "We have Stella, Beck's, Guinness, Bud Light," said Kara Sassone, the company's media relations specialist, as she rattles off the more popular labels. A cold one helps encourage employees to hang out at the office and build better working relationships according to the company. Free or not, beer, as with all good things, is best in moderation, especially at the office. Even so, it's a popular perk. "I'm sure if we were to get rid of the beer fridge here at HubSpot, the whole company would be up in arms," blogged one employee.[77]

DPR Construction and its Wine Bars. You can drink Merlot in all 17 of the Redwood City, California, based company offices, except for its Austin location, which has a saloon with beer on tap.[78]

You just can't mess with Beer Fridays. **F5 Networks**, once a scrappy Seattle startup and now a major provider of IT infrastructures, has once again left its competition in the dust with a refreshing, hoppy end-of-the-week tradition that has been around since its early days. "Beer Friday," one employee tells us, "is core to the culture of F5." Even those who don't drink are fans of Beer Friday, which they refer to as "Free peanuts, chips and veggies Friday." Refreshments aside, in an office of more than 750 people (and 2,000 around the globe), they also just appreciate the chance for a weekly get-together with co-workers from other departments.[79]

Grabbing a shot from the Jägermeister machine in the Z Bar, showing off their karaoke chops, getting uber-comfy in the Nightlight room—no, people aren't visiting Belltown's newest hot spot. It's

77. http://www.boston.com/jobs/news/articles/2011/11/06/employee_perks_hubspot_has_free_beer/
78. http://www.thefiscaltimes.com/Articles/2011/05/19/16-Company-Perks-That-Will-Make-You-Jealous.aspx#qcvJOSjM6q3jBsqP.99
79. http://blog.nwjobs.com/peoples_picks_2010/large_company/most_unusual_perks_1.html

Seattle agency **Zaaz**, a 150-person web design, analytics, and optimization firm.[80]

Grasshopper.com has a unique set of wheels. According to Taylor Aldredge:

> Our beer cart is a motorized cooler that can be driven around the office. Also, it comes with a caboose for more storage. We've used it for things like Beer Fridays, or to transport supplies to cookouts outside. Also, we've used it to introduce new employees around the office by having them sit on the caboose as someone drove them around. It's a great multi-purpose vehicle.

THE OTHER BREW

While there's a lot of good coffee in San Francisco, Blue Bottle is among the best. It's also kind of expensive. But luckily for **Zynga** employees, you can get free coffee from Blue Bottle at Zynga's "dog house" headquarters in San Francisco.[81]

A **Jetsetter** tab at the local coffee shop so Jetsetter teammates don't have to eat the cost of networking while working is an appreciated perk.

The headquarters for **Sophos** is located in an old bank branch office. The renovated head office features a 24/7 lounge complete with video games, foosball, billiards, and a self-serve lunch room with free coffee and tea.

80. ttp://blog.nwjobs.com/peoples_picks_2010/small_company/coolest_office_space.html?lid=710013
81. http://www.businessinsider.com/the-best-perks-in-tech-2012-7

IT'S JUST LUNCH

"We try to stay frugal—our office furniture is secondhand—but we cater lunch in at **ZocDoc** every day," says Allison Braley of ZocDoc. "We've tried to be really thoughtful about the perks we offer—lunch helps people get to know ZocDoc-ers from other departments. Aeron chairs don't."[82]

Submitted by Taylor Aldredge: "I'm the Ambassador of Buzz at **Grasshopper**, a virtual phone system for entrepreneurs. We have a Wii and Playstation 3 room, free healthy food and drinks all day, a pool table, and a green lunch program that gives people $5 a day towards their lunch." The $5 for lunch stood out, so I asked Taylor how that worked. "The $5 Green Lunch is pretty straightforward. Grasshopper provides $5/day through a house account at DiningIn.com. So, you can order food from one of the restaurants at a discount, and it all gets delivered to the office. This way nobody's driving for lunch, and you're saving money by getting lunch at $5 off."

The Tuck Shop in San Francisco's **Dropbox** office was designed specifically to be a space of comfort for all Dropbox employees. When you walk into the open-layout cafeteria, you will find decorative rugs, potted plants, a juice bar, and an in-house coffee roaster. You can easily get tucked away here during the more stressful days.[83]

PROVIDING HEALTHIER FOOD AND SNACKS

U.S. workers eat tons of sugary and fatty junk food, often because that's all they have time to scarf down between meetings. Though you can't be expected to single-handedly halt the U.S. culture's mad

---

82. http://mashable.com/2012/05/28/startup-perks-culture/
83. https://www.thedailymeal.com/eat/best-office-cafeterias-america-gallery/slide-2

rush into obesity, companies can make it easier for workers to make better choices, whether it's by making healthy foods more readily available or having a long enough lunch break so that fast food is only an option rather than a necessity.

From bins filled with free healthy snacks to tapping a keg at 4 p.m. every afternoon, **Digitas** offers employees a wide variety of perks and benefits to keep them energized.[84]

At **Morningstar**, they believe that even "the little things count," which is why the company provides employees with an egalitarian environment, free beverages, free bagels on Wednesday, and casual dress every day.[85]

Team members at **Realflow** make daily smoothies. The ritual every so often turns into a fun competition where taste and nutrition are the criteria used to judge the winner.

NYC PR Agency **Lippe Taylor** tries to offer employees the best of both worlds: financial benefits typically found only in big companies and the hands-on touch of hominess that comes with a smaller company. It feeds its employees early and often: from morning perk Mondays (breakfast spread of bagels, muffins, fresh fruit, and orange juice) to its signature Sweet Treat on Wednesdays. Creativity abounds with account executives pairing seasonal tie-ins with tasty treats—think mini milkshakes on National Milkshake Day and chips and salsa for Cinco de Mayo.[86]

DINNER IS SERVED

Take-home dinners are provided to employees at **Genentech**.

84. https://www.chicagobusiness.com/node/407056/printable/print
85. http://www.businessinsider.com/companies-with-awesome-perks-2012-10?op=1#ixzz2EBoyA9J1
86. https://www.prnewsonline.com/2012-top-places-to-work-in-pr-lippe-taylor-brand-communications/

Employees at **Facebook** can take home a free dinner or, if working late, their families can come in to eat with them, leading to a regular sight of children in the campus cafeteria.[87]

PAVLOV'S PAYDAY GOODNESS

Blue Buddha, a maker of custom jewelry, provides employees with premium chocolate on paydays. The General Operations Manager purchases the chocolate ahead of time and then distributes two pieces to each person. Sometimes employees pick up chocolate when they walk in and go past the manager's desk. Everyone has a physical "inbox," so the manager will put the chocolate in their inbox for people who aren't there on payday—a treat available to them on their next working day.

MILLENNIAL MOMENT

Millennials like munching. In 2017, *QSR Magazine* conducted a survey on how millennials were shaping the food industry. Among many data points, perhaps the most interesting were that 61 percent wished for more foods that reminded them of their grandmother's cooking and 69 percent desired meals that brought back memories of their childhood. An additional stat was that a staggering 81 percent of millennials said they enjoy exploring new cultures through their cuisine. Tickling the taste buds of this generation at work warrants food selections from both Granny Helen and ethnic food truck options.[88]

87. http://www.nytimes.com/2012/10/20/us/in-silicon-valley-perks-now-begin-at-home.html?pagewanted=all&_r=1&

88. https://www.qsrmagazine.com/news/study-millennials-continue-shaping-food-industry

CHAPTER 14

BUILDING: SHELTER

"It seems as if it was just a few years ago that we were taking people out of offices and putting them into cubicles. From there, the trend went to open work spaces, then hoteling, and then shared hoteling "cubes"—all driven by the need to keep real-estate costs low in a very acquisitions-oriented industry that's always streamlining. Now, more and more of our employees are working remotely. In many ways, that's a good thing. It gives people a lot more flexibility and freedom, and makes them happier about the job because they're able to put their lives together in ways that matter to them."

— Rebecca Ranninger, Chief HR Officer, Symantec

GIMME SHELTER

A key to driving employee engagement is Shelter. Pure and simple—space matters. It sets the stage for how you both work and interact on the job. Beyond functionality, the physical environment should be able to tell the story of the company. According to Mark Fidelman, "The best workplaces find a way to integrate their organization's culture and mission. In the future, these workspaces will also help your workforce become more effective. Workplaces will become adaptive—where physical objectives and software adapt to the working style of the organization and not the other way around. Work in the workplace will become more human and more results oriented."[89]

TO CUBE OR NOT TO CUBE?

The word cube has four letters. The traditional view is that it's a bad four-letter word. No one aspires to work in a cube. Stan's sister Mary Ann worked at a benefits consulting practice in Philadelphia in the early 90s. Positioned in an interior cube and bathed in fluorescent light, she would joke about the desire for an office. The senior team at the firm (all men) occupied them all. "No balls, no walls" was the inside joke.

Some workplaces mandate that there are no offices. **Zappos**, for example, is entirely a cube culture. Even the management team sits in an area affectionately dubbed as "Monkey Row." Other workplaces take the concept one step further. No offices or cubes, just rows of desks with no barriers like at the agency **Gyro**.

Maybe the answer is somewhere in between open and closed. Mary Lee Duff of **Interior Architects** chimes in:

---

89. https://www.forbes.com/sites/markfidelman/2012/05/24/
   microsofts-view-of-the-future-workplace-is-brilliant-heres-why-2/#2bfd8d777d7c

The traditional concept of the high panel Dilbert cubicle has definitely been diminishing. The drive today is for workplace settings to be more open and collaborative with a strong emphasis on flexibility. For some clients that means going into benching systems, for others it is simply lowering the panel walls and being able to offer greater control over how to reconfigure one's own space.

MOVING FROM "I" TO "WE"

Flexibility is key, but so is diversity. Here is an interesting insight by former **Steelcase** CEO, Jim Hackett. "Celebrate the shift of what we call the 'I' space to the 'we' space …. Space has to enable and empower information in ways we only imagine … across a continuum of I and we work…. [P]eople need a range of settings to accommodate focused, collaborative, and social work in both open and enclosed environments—in other words, a palette of place."

Let's have a look at a baker's dozen of companies who've tackled space (the "Final Frontier") with a little something extra.

OPEN AND FLEXIBLE BY DESIGN

Kayak.com has an open office environment. In the words of Paul English, "I sit out with the product managers. We hold design meetings at one another's desks throughout the day. We do design interaction like that, where everyone can hear and anyone can jump in. If anyone needs to make a private phone call, there are a few private offices, but our general philosophy is that an open environment facilitates intellectual intensity. Most engineers are introverted. Here, when people overhear a discussion, we encourage them to walk over and say, 'There's another way to do that.'"[90]

---

90. http://www.inc.com/magazine/20100201/the-way-i-work-paul-english-of-kayak_pagen_2.html

In an effort to foster collaboration among the 15 employees at brand communications firm **Trevelino/Keller**, there are no offices at the firm's HQ. The space at the King Plow Arts Center is open, both philosophically and physically. "There's no place to hide," says agency principal Dean Trevelino jokingly. Trevelino empowers his employees to make their own decisions to get the work done. "Everyone expects each other to work hard and do it with no ego."[91]

David Clarke, **BGT Partners** co-founder and managing partner, purposefully designed the office to have an open feel with "huddle rooms" for staff to verbalize any issues or ideas. "So often, IMs or e-mails get misconstrued. We want to encourage people to come back and forth and explore all other areas of the company if they're interested. We can only tell you to do so much."[92]

According to Jörg Pierach, **Fast Horse Inc.** founder and president, "We don't have offices, cubes or even assigned desks, which leads to greater collaboration while we're in the office, and allows people to be equally productive when they are away. Employees have the opportunity to work from virtually anywhere they have an Internet connection on a regular basis. And, during the summer, our office is closed on Fridays, allowing people to work from home in the morning and then get a jump on their summer weekend in the afternoon."[93]

TD Bank has the FlexWorkPlace pilot program to accommodate changing and flexible work patterns. It features redesigned floors that include more meeting rooms, no traditional offices, and a "collaborative" cafe where employees can meet and work in a comfortable and informal setting.

---

91. https://purplegoldfish.com/beyond-dilbert-the-importance-of-design-in-the-workplace-for-employee-engagement/

92. http://adage.com/article/best-places-to-work/places-work-media-marketing-bgt-partners/229314/

93. https://www.minnesotabusiness.com/innovative-horse

EAT, PRAY, WORK

According to some reports, the cost of stress in the workplace is approaching $300 billion per year in absenteeism, tardiness, poor performance, employee turnover, accidents, and stress-related workers' compensation claims. What's a brand to do?

The online marketplace **eBay** offers both prayer and meditation rooms. Employees can sit in silence—in minimalist rooms decorated in earth tones, accented with cushy pillows, floor mats, and fragrant flower buds—to catch a few critical moments of solitude and to decompress from the myriad stresses of a workday.[94]

No one at **PARTNERS+simons** has to leave the office to make a private phone call. Instead, they slip inside one of two large, soundproof tubes in the company's coffee and kitchen area where they can chat away. The South Boston ad agency has two cell phone booths that look like something out of the transporter room from "Star Trek." Trudy Almquist, CFO at the agency, said that employees were regularly using conference and meeting rooms for private calls to their spouses or their children's schools. "Conference room time was at a premium, and this was a better option," she said. "It's just a place to talk to your doctor, adoption agent, your spouse, or whatever you have going on in your life. It's to have a little privacy in a public place."[95]

Forget hours of toiling under harsh lights in a stiff chair or being trapped in a maze of confined spaces. At **Alberici's** headquarters, the light pours in through walls of windows, the chairs are ergonomically designed to draw out body heat, and the space is so open and sleek that it feels as if a library and modern art gallery hooked up. "It's a little overwhelming when you walk in," says project engineer Peter Nuernberger. A native prairie and a white wind turbine

94. http://www.cult-branding.com/business-life/articles-on-business-life/mindfulness-in-the-workplace/

95. http://www.boston.com/jobs/news/articles/2011/11/06/partners__simons_has_cell_phone_booths_for_privacy/

outside offer a preview of the building's environmentally friendly design. Inside, bamboo covers elevator walls, and employees dine on heart-healthy subsidized lunches. Everything whispers of the company's innovative culture—with an emphasis on whispers. In fact, the company even plays white noise throughout the day. "It is kind of like working in a library," says Jay Reiter, Director of Marketing.[96]

Shhh… **SAP Canada's** headquarters offers a quiet room for employees who need a quick break during the busy day.

WORKING TOWARD HOME

The professional services recruitment firm **Goodman Masson** doesn't just want to make a stable home for its employees—it wants to help them buy one too or pay off an existing mortgage. When an employee of this London-based financial services recruitment firm saves 20 percent of basic pay for three years, the company will add 33 percent to that deposit/lump sum saving—or 50 percent if the employee has included bonuses in the savings program too. All 135 company employees are eligible for this program.[97]

Employees of **Paramount Staffing** who are purchasing a home for the first time receive $5,000.[98]

KITCHEN CONFIDENTIAL

At **Clockwork Active Media Systems,** the best gathering of the day is the one that takes place every single morning. Clockwork has a large kitchen table that seats about 25 people. Every morning

---

96. https://www.stlmag.com/Great-Places-to-Work-January-2009/

97. https://www.employeebenefits.co.uk/issues/november-2016/
goodman-massons-benefits-package-serves-to-retain-and-engage-employees/

98. http://www.businessinsider.com/the-25-best-small-companies-to-work-for-right-now-2012-10?op=1#ixzz2E945CFga

the table is packed with employees starting their day with a cup of coffee and chatting with each other about the work that needs to happen that day. That organic kind of gathering speaks more to the strength of Clockwork's work culture than any holiday party ever could.[99]

Just three years ago, **HOK's** office space in St. Louis was a federal bankruptcy court with courtrooms that "looked like bad funeral-home chapels," recalls vice chairman Clark Davis. So, when executives decided to renew their lease at Met 1 and move all of their employees to one floor, the world-renowned architecture firm did what it does best: transform the space into one of the most environmentally friendly offices in St. Louis. "We essentially created a loft-quality space inside a 20-year-old building," says Davis. Now the office is an airy environment with a prime view of the Arch and Busch Stadium that everyone can share. Stationed in rows of desks, architects and designers debate blueprints for projects, including one in Saudi Arabia. "Almost everything we do is based on collaboration," says Davis, "so we wanted to encourage communication and bring people together." An open kitchen serves as a common meeting place. Glass-walled "huddle rooms" offer intimate spaces for employees to chat. Even 85-year-old founding partner Gyo Obata works inside a small cube surrounded by other creative minds.[100]

The young workforce at **Unruly**, average age 29, thinks jobs are good for personal growth. These would-be "Unrulies" earn more than the minimum wage, get the first crack at any jobs coming up and meanwhile, get to eat the same croissants as the boss. Christian d'Ippolito, Group Head of International Sales, says, "There's this energy in the company that makes everything exciting…. [T]here's a particular culture here, a tight sense of community and it's a lot of fun." Matt Cooke, CTO and a company founder, says, "It's very collaborative and social. We aren't dictating—we are inclusive, and small things make a big difference, like a big kitchen."[101]

XPLANE, which was founded in 1993, has an "Inspiration Wall"—a designated space in the office kitchen where employees can post anything they have created or want to share that inspires them. "It helps us express new ideas and personal findings which foster surprising connections, creative collaborations and, at its simplest, helps us all know each other better."[102]

SLEEPING ON THE JOB

At **AOL** headquarters in NYC, perks include access to NapQuest, a specialized room where employees can grab some winks in "nap pods" and relax in one of many electronic massage chairs.[103]

GARDEN PARTY

Southern Ohio Medical Center started a garden and invited the staff to plant their own vegetables or come pick them on their lunch break. Consisting of two small greenhouses and several large raised beds, the garden turns out kale, broccoli, tomatoes, Brussels sprouts, rhubarb, strawberries, and lettuce.[104]

LAGNIAPPE EXAMPLES: Beyond shelter, here are a couple of examples that address clothing:

Clothes Make the Banker: Employees at **Umpqua Bank** are given $500 TWICE per year to purchase professional clothing for work. The amount is then deducted from their paychecks until paid

---

101. https://www.thetimes.co.uk/?sunday

102. http://www.entrepreneur.com/article/220512

103. http://www.cbsnews.com/8301-505263_162-57451292/huffington-talks-sleep-overbooked-huffpost-nap-rooms/?tag=showDoorFlexGridRight;flexGridModule

104. http://www.worldatwork.org/waw/adimComment?id=58501

in full in as little as $10 per paycheck. The result is no credit card interest.[105]

Dress Code: The right atmosphere is important. At **BBS Technologies** that means striving to replicate the freedom and intellectual excitement of a college campus. The dress code? "You must wear clothes," CEO Rick Pleczko said. Otherwise, Pleczko adds, he wants everyone to feel comfortable at the software company as he tries to combine a casual atmosphere with a professional environment. "We care what you produce and deliver, but not so much how you look."[106]

105. http://money.cnn.com/magazines/fortune/bestcompanies/2011/snapshots/25.html
106. http://www.chron.com/business/top-workplaces/article/Paid-volunteer-time-dogs-at-work-and-other-perks-2254147.php

MILLENNIAL MOMENT

Good vibes only. The millennial generation cares highly about what their workspace looks and feels like. **Mindspace**, a co-working space company, and the research firm **One Poll** have determined that a fifth of the millennial generation has admitted to rejecting a potential employer simply because of the look of the workspace. **Capital One's** 2017 Workplace Study found that office design cannot be a "one size fits all" approach. The current consensus is that there has to be a balance between open-floor-collaborative-heavy plans and the outdated, soul-crushing cubicle. Too much openness in a floor plan results in a complete lack of privacy and too much enclosed wall space is starved of innovation. The answer? Ask your employees of all generations what their ideal work space is and, rest assured, they will tell you.[107]

---

107. https://allwork.space/

CHAPTER 15

BUILDING: TRANSPARENCY

"There are three requirements of a great workplace: 1) Like the people you work with, 2) Do work that is meaningful and 3) Trust the management."

— Dave Hitz of NetApp

HOW DO YOU BUILD TRUST?

Buffer has a unique response to that question. "Default to transparency" is the phrase that has become rooted within the Buffer company culture. Since 2013, transparency has been integrated into the core values with beliefs like "always state your thoughts immediately and with honesty" and "use transparency as a tool to help others." Buffer is well known for the ease of public access to information such as the salary of every single employee, the individual equity formula, and the company's diversity statistics filtered by department, gender, ethnicity, and age.

In 2013, transparency became officially integrated as a guiding principle. Maurice Cherry, Marketing, Design, and Communications Lead at Glitch, interviewed Courtney Seiter, Director of People for Buffer in January of 2018. Courtney provided an interesting perspective to the culture of Buffer due to being a user of their services prior to employment. Courtney claimed that Buffer was her top choice for a social media manager and the solution for her to engage with her audience at the most effective times of day. Upon using Buffer more frequently, she started to gravitate from just the product to learning more about the company's culture from the culture slide deck and the core values that ran the company. Courtney said, "So yeah, I was kind of a fangirl early on."

Later in the interview, Courtney said that there is a "transparency dashboard" where anyone can see several different types of trends such as the upward and downward movement of revenue and other financial reports. There have been cases where, in the spirit of true transparency, individuals have seen the moving trends on the dashboard and actually blogged about what they would do to bring the numbers back up. "... we love that. We read those with such interest and often we'll reach out to those people," said Courtney.

Perhaps an even more interesting side effect of transparency is the job pool. Courtney said, "When we made salaries transparent, for the next open role, we had double the applicants for it. I think that's a pretty strong sign that folks feel aligned with what we're up to."[108]

Let's look for additional transparency guidance from India's **HCL Technologies** and Brazil's **Semco.**

Vineet Nayar, CEO of HCL Technologies touched on trust in his bestselling book, *Employees First, Customers Second.*[109] In the book, he outlined four ways that transparency builds trust:

1. Transparency ensures that every stakeholder knows the company's vision and understands how their contribution assists the organization in achieving its goals. Working in an environment without transparency is like trying to solve a jigsaw puzzle without knowing what the finished picture is supposed to look like.

2. It ensures that every stakeholder has a deep personal commitment to the aims of the organization.

3. Gen Y members expect transparency as a given. They post their life stories in public domains; they expect nothing less in their workplaces.

4. In a knowledge economy, we want customers to be transparent with us, to share their ideas, their vision and their strategies for solving core problems. Why would customers be transparent with us if we don't trust employees enough to be transparent with them?

---

108. https://open.buffer.com/transparency-timeline/

109. http://www.forbes.com/sites/karlmoore/2012/05/14/employees-first-customers-second-why-it-really-works-in-the-market/

Brazil's Semco is a great example of a democratic open environment with minimal hierarchy. The group of companies is headed up by CEO Ricardo Semler. According to British management guru Charles Handy, "The way he works—letting his employees choose what they do, where and when they do it, and even how they get paid—is too upside-down for most managers."

The company operates as an open book. In Semler's words:

> Semco has no official structure. It has no organizational chart. There's no business plan or company strategy, no two-year or five-year plan, no goal or mission statement, no long-term budget. The company often does not have a fixed CEO. There are no vice presidents or chief officers for information technology or operations. There are no standards or practices. There's no human resources department. There are no career plans, no job descriptions or employee contracts. No one approves reports or expense accounts. Supervision or monitoring of workers is rare indeed .... Most important, success is not measured only in profit and growth.

Let's look at another baker's dozen of companies that go the extra mile to be open and transparent.

OPEN BY DESIGN

A visionary corporation, **W. L. Gore** is built from a blueprint that its founder refers to as a "lattice" (as opposed to a "ladder"). There is no visible hierarchy at Gore, and there are no job titles. In fact, there are no bosses. Instead, there are leaders who achieve their positions by gaining followers. Business goals are established by consensus. Gore's internal "structure" was put into place in 1958 by co-founder Bill Gore, an ex-DuPont exec who believed, "leaders should be chosen by the people who follow them."[110]

If you join **Marina Maher Communications**, don't expect a title on your business card. "In our 28+ years, we've never put titles on business cards," said Maree Prendergast, managing director-human resources and talent. "We always thought that limits people." In fact, the company's philosophy is "good ideas come from everywhere," said Marina Maher, founder of the PR agency.[111]

Rule #1 of their 5 Core Values at open company **Atlassian** is No Bullshit. The Australian company embraces transparency wherever at all practical, and sometimes where impractical. All information, both internal and external, is public by default. "We are not afraid of being honest with ourselves, our staff, and our customers."[112]

Feedback Plus has an open ledger policy for employees. They can read the company's financial statements any time they wish. Their compensation is based upon their work teams and the company's performance vs. the annual goals and action plans they've collectively developed.[113]

Of course, it may not be feasible for every company to have an open ledger policy, but it is important that, whatever the size of the organization, each employee knows where they are going and how they're supposed to get there.

Employees at **Catalyst Studios** say founder Jason Rysavy's focus on finding like-minded colleagues and challenging projects is what makes the firm a fun place to work. "My job and the job of the leadership here is to make sure the projects we're bringing in

110. http://www.fastcompany.com/32710/you-have-no-boss

111. http://adage.com/article/special-report-best-places-to-work-2012/
    ad-age-s-places-work-11-marina-maher-communication/233647/

112. http://atlassian.com/

113. http://www.careercast.com/career-news/keys-great-corporate-culture-improving-employee-engagement

are satisfying for people to work on." The firm looks for challenging, unique projects in need of solutions. Rysavy said, "We tend to get these bastard-child projects that no one knows how to deal with, and we help figure it out." Over time, the firm has learned to turn down work that won't excite the agency's passionate problem-solvers. "The more you say no to the stuff that is clearly not a good fit for the people we have, the more the good stuff comes along," Rysavy said. "We made a lot of money early on, but we did a lot of stuff that didn't get us anywhere." Delivering a product that clients and users can enjoy and that was satisfying to build is a reward beyond the "smoke and mirrors" that other agencies use to keep their employees happy.[114]

Talent Plus + holds monthly business update meetings. Management shares financials with all employees in the spirit of transparency.

AN OPEN DOOR

At **Flour Bakery + Cafe**, none of the bakery manager offices have doors and all have anonymous suggestion boxes. "We try to create all sorts of ways to get feedback from the staff," says General Manager Aaron Constable.[115]

Rand Corporation offers an open-door policy at all levels of the organization. Anyone can make an appointment to meet with the CEO, Executive VP, or any of the other VP staff. The company leadership host small group lunch meetings as well as coffee get-togethers for open Q&A.[116]

114. http://www.bizjournals.com/twincities/

115. http://www.boston.com/jobs/news/articles/2011/11/06/the_best_employers_appreciate_their_workers/

116. http://labusinessjournal.com/

OPENNESS ONE STEP AT A TIME

AnswerLab's CEO schedules Walk & Talks with every employee. These one-on-one check-ins provide employees with an individual opportunity to share any concerns or brilliant ideas they have with the CEO directly. Combining wellness with one-on-ones helps achieve two important objectives simultaneously. Meeting outside the office and getting physical helps eliminate the nerves and intimidation employees might normally experience when connecting with higher-ups.[117]

Team One believes its "management by walking" practice and team camaraderie help maintain the culture at the agency.[118]

Doug Conant, former CEO of **Campbell's Soup Company**, took purposeful steps to being visible and promote good health at Campbell›s. Ten thousand steps per day to be exact in order to stay connected to employees.[119]

Everyone at the **Max Borges Agency** has the ability to discuss anything with anyone at the agency, where its "do not knock" policy is taken seriously. Taking that one step further, the company recently sponsored a four-week in-office communications course that was taught during regular business hours. It was based on the book *People Styles at Work*, and its purpose was to enhance everyone's ability to effectively communicate with co-workers, clients, and family.[120]

OVERTIME EXTRA

The **DRP Group** recognizes long hours working on videos, events, print, and digital productions. "If the client pays for overtime, the

117. http://www.greatplacetowork.com/storage/documents/publications/top-ten-people-practices.pdf

118. http://adage.com/article/special-report-best-places-to-work-2012/team-12-ad-age-s-places-work-list/233662/

119. https://hbr.org/2016/07/the-connection-between-employee-trust-and-financial-performance

120. http://www.prnewsonline.com/

team member will get 50 percent of what is charged." The policy has allowed some staff to make 30 percent extra per year.[121]

OPEN AND SECURE

National Instruments (NI) puts their employees first. "When other employers lay off in droves, NI hangs on, relying on cash they have consistently put away for the inevitable economic recession." This quote was shared by National Instruments Digital Hardware Engineer on Glassdoor.

According to the **David Martin Agency**, "We are different from other companies in our industry as we are salaried. By removing the commission-based compensation usually found in this industry, it allows all of us to enjoy the success of the individual performances. We celebrate our successes by announcing them company-wide. We share financial bonuses across all employees. Our philosophy is that sharing successes make our jobs even better!"[122]

STANDING UP FOR EMPLOYEES

Bad customers beware. **ING Direct** (now part of Capital One) stands up to protect their employees. The bank has an operating strategy based on a strong, effective culture that is selective of prospective customers. It also requires the periodic "firing" of customers. At ING Direct, thousands are fired every month. This strategy is especially important when customers "abuse" employees or make unreasonable demands on them.[123]

The rapidly growing **Belvedere Trading** gives both traders and its information technology staff opportunities to share ideas and take

121. http://www.thesundaytimes.co.uk/sto/

122. http://www.thesundaytimes.co.uk/sto/

123. https://hbswk.hbs.edu/item/10-reasons-to-design-a-better-corporate-culture

on new roles. "We want for every employee to feel an ownership in the firm, that they're going to have an impact on what we do," says Thomas Hutchinson, Belvedere Trading president. It's a flat structure," he adds. "No matter where they come from, ideas are taken with a serious attitude." Reflecting that flat structure, everyone in the firm, including interns, receives a bonus twice a year, which ranges from 5 to 200 percent of the employee's salary.[124]

KEEPING IT ON THE LEVEL

Hilcorp's annual bonus is universal. There is a single set of targets and every employee is rewarded with the same percentage of his or her salary. The company shells out a maximum 60 percent bonus each year and has averaged 35 percent during the past five years.[125]

If **Integrated Project Management Company** exceeds its monthly profit targets, all employees receive the same bonus amount, regardless of position.

MAKING EMPLOYEES OWNERS

Wenck Associates is a 100 percent employee-owned company, backed by robust contributions to the plan and has enjoyed healthy growth to the value of the company stock. The ESOP program and contributions provided are differentiators, helping Wenck attract and retain members. From a financial performance standpoint, the company has an open book policy, sharing financial information monthly and at events throughout the year. Wenck provides a "self-directed training account" program, which allows employees to obtain additional development and training throughout the year to further their education and chase their dreams. There are many

124. http://www.chicagorealestatedaily.com/article/20110402/ISSUE02/304029982/
    best-places-to-work-no-20-belvedere-trading-llc#ixzz23ecl6mZ6

125. http://www.chron.com/

opportunities to grow, to be flexible, and to have a balanced life. **The result**: employees turning around and doing great things.[126]

Shares went to all 82 staff at **Mount Anvil**, allocated according to length of service, starting at £5,000. For Killian Hurley, the chief executive and co-founder, it was "the right thing to do. There are lots of good companies, but we want to be excellent and to do that, you need engaged, positive people delivering excellent customer service. The share incentive is one of the little steps we can control; we are delighted to do it."[127]

The egalitarian ethos of the wholly employee-owned architecture practice **Make** is reflected in an annual profit share for all 100+ staff. Everyone is a partner, and all feel fairly treated. It stands to reason that as owners, the staff insists on equitable pay.[128]

LAGNIAPPE: Semco has an interesting program. You don't need to wait until you're old to enjoy your retirement. The idea is that you can take advantage of it once a week, from any age. The "Retire a little bit" project was created based on a life-cycle analysis. [According to Semco] in any analysis that we undertake, we will see that we have money when we don't have time to enjoy it, time when we no longer have financial certainty, and the ability to enjoy nature and sports when we no longer have the health to do so. The program allows the person to do what they plan to do when they retire, once a week, like an art course, play sports in the afternoon, or simply spend the day with their kids. The employee will have the option not to work one day a week, replacing this day in the future, after they retire, with a proportional salary.[129]

---

126. https://www.bizjournals.com/twincities/
127. https://www.thetimes.co.uk/
128. https://www.thetimes.co.uk/
129. http://www.semco.com.br/en/content.asp?content=4&contentID=570

MILLENNIAL MOMENT

We all remember 2008 and the hardships that ensued for the entire country. From the millennials' perspective, 2008 and the years following were when their opinions about the world were being shaped and, for many, those were their first years of employment. For the younger Gen Yers, those were the years they watched their parents and other relatives lose almost everything due to layoffs from companies their families had been loyal to for decades. Goldman Sachs released a study specifically concentrated on how 2008 affected the trajectory of the entire generation. Because of the recession, millennials have taken a cautious perspective on any big personal financial decisions, but more importantly they have taken a second look at the finances of the companies they work for. Trust in "the man," i.e. businesses, took a significant decrease for millennials during this time frame. Organizations would do well to keep in mind the importance of transparency to this generation. Keep millennials informed and calm through openness.[130]

---

130. https://www.entrepreneur.com/article/314156

CHAPTER 16

BUILDING: WELLNESS

"If there's a fountain of youth, it is probably physical activity. Research has shown benefits to every organ system in the body. So the problem isn't whether it's a good idea. The problem is how to get people to do more of it."

— Dr. Toni Yancey, Author of *Instant Recess*

WORKPLACE WELLNESS

Getting to the heart of your employees involves wellness, little extras designed to support healthy behavior in the workplace and improve health outcomes. Without health, we have nothing. It's an easy concept to grasp. More than just health, wellness is also about enhancing productivity.

Why is Wellness so basic? Max Borges of the **Max Borges Agency** breaks it down simply. "When you feel good physically," the triathlete says, "you feel good mentally." The South Florida company, which does public relations for the consumer electronics industry, offers employee benefits such as an on-site gym, fitness classes, and reimbursement for athletic competition entry fees.[131]

Conversely, employees without a sense of wellness tend to take excessive sick days and suffer from low job satisfaction. Leaders at Canada's **Halton Healthcare** were faced with these exact issues. They found a solution in "Kailo," a decidedly psycho-social framework for staff wellness that was developed at Mercy Medical Center in Northern Iowa. Kailo, an ancient word meaning whole, pulls into balance all aspects of health and well-being, including social, emotional, spiritual, and physical elements. "We wanted to build trust and improve relationships among employees. Kailo offered proven approaches to demonstrate respect and value for all employees, regardless of their current health practices, and allowed us also to promote humor, fun, and play in the workplace," says Anna Rizzotto, Halton's Kailo Coordinator.

Times of caring and sharing among co-workers were dubbed "Kailo" moments. Staff embraced all the benefits of Kailo, including "Kailo-to-Go" in-services, the Kailo Treat Kart, the Kailo First Aid

---

131. http://www.dailyfinance.com/2010/12/22/successful-companies-gain-profits-by-adding-employee-benefits/

Basket, and the ever-popular mini-massage. "The feel-good impact of mini-massage appears to surpass all other program offerings!"[132]

TWO PATHS DIVERGE

As an employer you have two choices. Ignore wellness and pay a hefty premium (pun intended) or take action.

Let's look at a baker's dozen of companies in the latter category with organizations that demonstrate the ability to go the extra mile to promote workplace wellness.

FINANCIAL INCENTIVES

At **Kahler Slater**, a Milwaukee-based architectural design firm, employees have access to health coaches and risk assessments. Individuals who meet health goals are rewarded with a discount of $720 off their annual health premiums. In addition, the firm sponsors a Wellness Committee that creates promotional and competitive activities to keep its 125 employees engaged. The committee works on three firm-wide activities per year, including charity weight loss challenges and events such as a "Fast Food Challenge," which encourages employees to avoid fast food for a month.[133]

The wellness program at **Borshoff** includes subsidized yoga classes onsite, free pedometers, educational seminars, and incentives to promote healthy living and positive work/life balance. Those who set and reach wellness goals receive $50 off their monthly insurance premium. The program has 91 percent employee participation.[134]

132. http://www.qwqhc.ca/knowledge-exchange-archived-05.aspx

133. http://www.greatplacetowork.net/publications-and-events/blogs-and-news/547

134. http://www.prnewsonline.com/

To encourage employees to consider alternative transportation, **Nature's Path Foods** offers employees $500 each year to spend on physical activities, which could include the purchase of a bicycle for commuting, and it supports employees with secure bike storage and onsite shower facilities.

WINTER WELLNESS

There may be no such thing as a free lunch, but at **Anadarko Petroleum Corp.**, there is a free flu shot. Recently, an in-house doctor started at the top of the company's 30-story office tower in The Woodlands and over three weeks worked his way down, floor by floor, giving injections to nearly 1,900 employees at their desks—at no charge.[135]

Everyone at **First Response Finance** gets a "winter bag" packed with lip balm, an ice scraper, porridge, throat soothers, and honey and lemon to see them through the darkest months.[136]

GYM DANDY

Some organizations have a company gym. Others may subsidize or pay for gym fees. **Reebok** took this to the next level in 2010 by converting a brick warehouse at Reebok's headquarters into an employee-exclusive CrossFit "box" (workout center) named CrossFit One with six coaches and extensive equipment. About 425 employees at Reebok are taking part. This benefit reinforces the company's new mission: to get consumers moving. Participants lost over 4,000 pounds collectively during its first year.[137]

135. http://www.chron.com/
136. https://www.thetimes.co.uk/
137. http://corporate.reebok.com/en/about_reebok/Reebok CrossFit.asp

In Canada, **Accenture** has an interesting perk for traveling employees. It offers a unique "Athletic Minded Traveler" program that includes reimbursement for use of hotel health clubs.[138]

Great Little Box Company Ltd. has a corporate HQ that features a fully-equipped onsite fitness facility (with subsidized membership and personal training services), outdoor sand volleyball court, book exchange library, outdoor gazebo, rooftop deck, and even a dock for employees who wish to commute by kayak to Mitchell Island.[139]

Arc'Teryx Equipment Inc. provides employees with a wide range of onsite amenities including a fitness facility with an indoor bouldering cave.[140]

Gentle Giant Moving Company, a small business based in Boston, has a unique wellness benefit. John Zimmer, an in-house chiropractor and renowned CrossFit trainer, works every day with movers, office staff, and executives in the custom-built CrossFit gym right inside of their warehouse. According to Mitch Curtis of Gentle Giant, the company has always focused on strength and fitness, but over the past few years, John has helped ingrain it even further in their company culture. Everyone finds his services to be a HUGE benefit, as daily gym access with a personal trainer can be quite expensive."[141]

THE FULL MONTY

Whole Foods pays 100 percent of healthcare premiums for its employees.

---

138. http://www.eluta.ca/top-employer-accenture

139. http://eluta.ca/

140. http://www.outsideonline.com/

141. http://www.gentlegiant.com/Moving-Companies.aspx

Alterian pays 99 percent of the premiums and covers the deductibles of its medical plan and gives employees a $50 monthly health stipend that can be used for health club memberships, vitamins, and such.[142]

Since 1988, **Starbucks** has offered full healthcare benefits to eligible full and part-time partners. All employees (yes, even part-timers who work 20 hours a week) are eligible for health insurance benefits. In addition, the Thrive Wellness Campaign inspires Starbucks partners to take advantage of wellness opportunities and lead active, healthy lives, which, long term, will help sustain comprehensive benefits at Starbucks.[143]

REIMBURSEMENTS AND STIPENDS

Employees at **Nerland** are reimbursed their entry fee once they successfully complete any sort of athletic achievement, such as a marathon, 5K, sprint-tri, or bike race.[144]

Kashi offers employees health-insurance discounts for competing in sports leagues and a $400 stipend to spend on "natural healthy-lifestyle" products like a surfboard or cooking classes.[145]

LEVERAGING PROGRAMS AND ACTIVITIES

Groups of employees at **Root Learning** gather for yoga every Thursday evening in the company lobby.

Savings.com supports a healthy lifestyle. The office offers the P90x program, a 90-day commitment to health, body, mind, and energy

---

142. http://www.chicagobusiness.com/article/20110402/ISSUE02/304029983/
       best-places-to-work-no-19-alterian-inc#ixzz23ec6nxuQ
143. http://assets.starbucks.com/assets/7343fbbdc87845ff9a000ee009707893.pdf
144. http://www.outsideonline.com/magazine
145. http://www.outsideonline.com/magazine

reserves. The company paid for the employees to get the P90x videos, which have become part of the company's library of books and DVDs. Savings.com provides a catered lunch for all employees every Tuesday. In addition, it has a fully stocked kitchen with snacks, drinks, and health conscious foods.

Beyond building design and construction projects at **Clayco**, many employees build toned bodies in a decked-out gym—complete with a personal trainer on the payroll. And after squeezing a quick workout into the day, they can shower off in bathrooms stocked with hairspray, Tums, mouthwash, floss, and more. Trainer and wellness director Brian Imholz believes he's the only full-time trainer in the country with such a job. About one-third of Clayco's 350 local employees regularly work out at the gym. "This is a place where you want to perform as well as you can, because you want to work for a company that takes care of you," says IT director Tom Dutton. When Dutton started at Clayco more than a year ago, he weighed 314 pounds. But he began regularly hitting the gym, drawing inspiration from quotes by Einstein and da Vinci painted on the company's walls. Now he glides on the elliptical machine while answering emails. So far, he's lost 104 pounds.[146]

GOING THE EXTRA MILE FOR WELLNESS

As part of its employee support network, the fast-growing energy company **NuStar** makes the corporate jet available in times of crisis. In 2010, when an employee working on a construction project in the Caribbean needed medical attention for a pre-existing ailment, NuStar jetted him back to the States to see his personal physician. The company also dispatches the plane when needed to send employees to support a coworker in need—flying employees from

---

146. https://www.stlmag.com

headquarters, say, to support a colleague in another location who had a death in the family.

Liberty Mutual offers Best Doctors. This free and confidential service is invaluable during those times when an employee or a family member receives a serious medical diagnosis. Through this program, founded by doctors affiliated with Harvard Medical School, you can consult with some of the world's top specialists to gain the insight and additional information needed to help confirm diagnosis and choose an appropriate treatment.[147]

At **Dixon Schwabl**, a Victor, New York, based advertising and public relations firm, many of the company's 82 employees began considering whether or not to decline health benefits altogether rather than take on higher rates. In response, the firm introduced a sliding scale benefit for health and dental insurance. For employees with the lowest annual salaries, the firm covers the majority of health-care costs. Those making the highest salaries pick up more of the cost, with top earners paying up to 100 percent of premiums.[148]

Balance is enforced at **BGT Partners**. To further encourage a friendly workplace, employees are expected to say "hi" every morning and "goodbye" every night. BGT does it during reasonable hours, no less. According to CEO and co-founder David Clarke, all offices recognize a fairly strict 9-to-6 work schedule. "Our managers will walk around and kick people out if they're in the office any later. We want people to take care of themselves, and if you're not happy that's gonna start hurting your work."[149]

Kaiser Permanente of Southern California sponsors bi-weekly farmer's markets at their campuses. The markets have included cooking demonstrations by Kaiser Permanente in the past.

147. http://reviews.greatplacetowork.com/liberty-mutual-insurance
148. http://www.greatplacetowork.net/publications-and-events/blogs-and-news/547
149. http://adage.com/article/best-places-to-work/places-work-media-marketing-bgt-partners/229314/

MILLENNIAL MOMENT

Gallup Workplace shared in late 2016 that millennials specifically desire jobs that promote their personal well-being. More than that, Gallup defines wellness as encompassing five different factors: purpose, social, financial, community, and physical. Unfortunately, Gallup and Healthways have discovered that the Y generation is the least likely of all generations to thrive in every one of the five wellness elements. At the time of this study, only five percent of employed millennials were thriving in all five of the elements, and only seven percent of workers in all generations combined were doing the same. The solution? Get to know your employees. Find the time and the process to discuss which of the five components your company is not fulfilling for them.[150]

CHAPTER 17

BUILDING: TIME AWAY

"Vacation days are like aspirin.
They only work if you take them."

— David Murphy

THE IMPORTANCE OF GETTING AWAY

A recent survey polled over 200 employees from 98 companies to find out what rewards they valued the most. "Across all ages and cultures, time off was absolutely number one," according to Cindy Ventrice, author of *Make Their Day! Employee Recognition that Works.*

Time away from the office is not only valued by employees, it's regenerative. Yet, Americans work an average of 47 hours weekly and average just two weeks of vacation a year.[151] Those 10 days put us dead last compared to all other developed countries.

Matt Kalinowski, CEO of **Kronos**, a management software and services company, shared the business's personal story on the importance of time away. On December 18, 2015, Kronos announced a new policy: unlimited vacation. Through intense research done by the HR department and Matt himself, Kronos decided to take the leap and, through a company-wide video Matt stated, "Thank you for creating an environment where we trust each other so much that we can take a step like this."

Interestingly enough, the response was not all celebratory clapping and cheering. There was a minority group of managers and other workers whose complaints "fell into three buckets," as Matt says. For a small group of managers, there was concern that this new policy would make their responsibilities that much more difficult when it came to the possibility of employees taking excessive time off. The blurred lines of "how much vacation is too much vacation" caused more stress than relief.

The second group of employees were upset because they looked at unused vacation hours as cash in their pocket. With this new pol-

---

151. https://www.cnbc.com/2018/07/05/heres-how-many-paid-vacation-days-the-typical-american-worker-gets-.html

icy, would they receive the compensation they "deserved" for not taking those precious vacation days?

The third and final group of people who were not thrilled about the change were those who operated on a tenure system. To an employee who had stayed with Kronos for 15 years, it seemed quite unfair that now a rookie would get the same opportunity for vacation time as the veterans. All valid points.

Kronos handled each complaint separately. While groups two and three were handled through informal conversations with Matt and the HR department, the managers in group one were consoled by being provided training and individual coaching to work through this grandiose change. Keep in mind that Kronos still wanted to have hard data on the effectiveness of unlimited vacation, so managers were asked to continue keeping track of their team's time off. This way, they could measure the results and see how the policy helped or hurt.

Now that the policy is in full swing, Kronos has enjoyed bearing the fruit. They have successfully created a culture where managers encourage their employees to take a day or two off if they notice they have not done so in a while. A few cool stories have come from the new policy. One employee took several weeks to ride in a motorcycle fundraiser that spanned over 48 states. Another employee was able to follow her daughter as she traveled with her show group performing Annie across cities. It is no surprise that as 2016 wrapped up, employees on average took 2.6 more vacation days per year and, financially speaking, 2016 was Kronos' best year yet. It pays to give your employees freedom and time off.[152]

Let's look at a baker's dozen of companies who place an emphasis on enabling employees to take time away from the office.

---

152. https://hbr.org/2017/11/the-ceo-of-kronos-on-launching-an-unlimited-vacation-policy

Managers at design firm **McMurry** receive quarterly reports that indicate how much PTO their employees have taken along with their unused inventory. Employees are encouraged to take time off by their managers, while blogs and stories by the CEO reinforce the importance of time away.

Why it's great: Making managers accountable for their team's time off helps ensure that workload is evenly distributed among teams, and that employees have the mental and physical energy they need to bring their best selves to work.

Why you should try it: Unused vacation time costs employees and employers. Not taking vacation is shown to be detrimental to an employee's health and productivity, and yet many employees report losing unused vacation time.[153]

PAID, PAID VACATION

The CEO of Denver-based Internet start-up **FullContact API** said in a market that is competitive for top talent, he wants to keep his employees happy and refreshed. The flip-flop wearing founder offers his employees $7,500 for what he calls "paid, paid vacation," however there are rules. "One, you actually have to take a vacation to get the money," Bart Lorang said. "Two, you have to disconnect from work, so that means no calls, no emails, no tweets, no work of any kind." Lorang admitted he has trouble following his rules. "I suck at it," he said. He has a picture with his fiancée Sarah at Egypt's great pyramids. Lorang is checking his email in the shot. Not surprisingly, employees said they loved having FullContact pick up the tab for their vacations. It's a real break for your brain. You come back refreshed and reinvigorated and more excited about the stuff

---

153. http://greatplacetowork.com/

you were working on when you left," said Robbie Jack, a FullContact API employee.[154]

Evernote recently changed their vacation policy to give people unlimited vacation. Employees can take as much time as they want, as long as they get their job done. In the words of former CEO Phil Libin, "If you want to take time off, talk to your team, but we're still measuring you on the same thing, which is, did you accomplish something great? Frankly, we want to treat employees like adults, and we don't want being in the office to seem like a punishment. We always try to ask whether a particular policy exists because it's a default piece of corporate stupidity that everyone expects you to have, or does it actually help you accomplish something? And very often you realize that you don't really know why you're doing it this way, so we just stop doing it." Has the unlimited vacation policy worked? "So far. We had to modify it slightly because one of the first things I started worrying about is whether people would actually take less vacation. I don't want people not to take any vacation because that's just bad for them, and it's bad for me. You're not going to get a lot of work out of someone if they haven't taken a vacation in a while. So, we started rewarding people for taking at least a week at a time on a real trip by giving them $1,000 spending money. That seems to be going well."[155]

MILESTONE REWARDS

A passport is required for this benefit. **New Belgium Brewery** rewards employees with a trip to Belgium with co-founder Kim Jordan on their fifth anniversary.

---

154. http://news.yahoo.com/blogs/abc-blogs/boss-gives-employees-7-500-vacations-143431561--abc-news-topstories.html

155. http://www.nytimes.com/2012/04/08/business/phil-libin-of-evernote-on-its-unusual-corporate-culture.
    html?pagewanted=1&_r=1

Employees at the consulting firm **Mark G. Anderson** enjoy an all-expense paid trip to one of the Seven Wonders of the World for their ten-year anniversary.

UK IT hosting provider **UKFast** provides a holiday allowance from 20 to 30 days. In the case of wedding bells in a given year, newly-weds get five extra days.[156]

Employees at **Element212** get three weeks of vacation to start and their wedding anniversary off.[157] [However, they are not responsible for reminding their employees of their anniversaries!]

If unlimited vacation is not incentive enough, after five years of working for **Red Frog Events**, employees are rewarded for their loyalty with a four-week, full-paid trip to Africa, Asia, Europe, or South America for them and a friend. It's no wonder they have 750 applicants apply for an open position there.[158]

EXTERNSHIPS

Bain & Company offers several opportunities for employees to take a break from demanding roles to help them sustain long-term careers at Bain. These include leaves of absence pr externships where employees can enrich their business knowledge by taking up to six months to work for another company.

Bank of Canada allows employees to work on exchange with other central banks and finance organizations.[159]

---

156. https://www.thetimes.co.uk/
157. http://element212.com/
158. http://www.theglobeandmail.com/report-on-business/careers/career-advice/
four-unique-employee-benefits-youve-never-heard-of/article4620730/
159. http://eluta.ca/

SABBATICALS

Kimpton is in the business of pampering guests, and it doesn't skimp on its staff either. The San Francisco-based operator of luxury boutique hotels provides one-month paid sabbaticals to managers and executive chefs who have been with the company for seven years.[160]

Employees at New York-based **Deloitte** don't have to sacrifice their life's dream for their careers because they enjoy the benefit of sabbatical leave. Deloitte offers four unpaid weeks off to do whatever they wish, and three to six months (yes, months) of partially paid leave to volunteer or pursue a career-enhancing opportunity.

Every seven years, designer Stefan **Sagmeister** closes his New York studio for a year-long sabbatical to rejuvenate and refresh their creative outlook. He believes the value of time off is often overlooked.[161]

Morningstar employees are eligible for generous sabbaticals. Six weeks paid time off every four years. In addition, employees can "take as much time as they want" for vacation. Rather than seeing that as a perk, employees were confused and tended not to take enough time. Now, the company specifies that the open vacation policy is defined as, "at least three weeks off."[162]

Alcool NB Liquor offers a self-funded leave program that lets employees defer a portion of their salary and take extended time off for up to one year with pay.[163]

---

160. http://www.crainsnewyork.com/gallery/20091207/FEATURES/120209998/9

161. http://www.youtube.com/watch?v=MNuOmTQdFjA

162. http://www.dailyfinance.com/2011/08/24/companies-that-treat-workers-right-get-good-karma-right-back/

163. http://www.chicagobusiness.com/article/20120331/ISSUE02/120329728/why-your-perks-arent-working

GENEROUS ALLOWANCES

Right out of the gate, **KPMG** offers five weeks off in year one of employment.[164]

Employees get twenty-five vacation days from **Strava** right from day one.

Media Temple is a web hosting and software application services company. After only your third year of service, you are eligible to take a full month of paid vacation to renew and rejuvenate efforts.

The biomedical software provider **5AM Solutions** offers eight weeks of vacation after 10 years of service, the ability to telecommute at least once a week, and three paid days a year to volunteer.[165]

164. http://www.thecareerrevolution.com/2008/03/most-unusual-company-perksscuba-diving.html

165. http://washingtonian.com/

MILLENNIAL MOMENT

Raised with computers, smartphones, and iEverythings, the millennials have been "online" since before they could legally vote. With an upbringing centered around connectivity to the entire world, it is almost impossible for this generation to completely unplug from their jobs. This is now a 24/7 culture where the expectation lies on emails sent at 10 p.m. and "calling to check in" during scheduled vacations. Time away is perhaps even more important for millennials than any other generation before them simply because they are the generation most likely to feel guilt for taking time off at all. Project Time Off released a crucial statistic: 30 percent of millennials do not take time off because they want to show true dedication to their job in comparison with 15 percent of baby boomers who do not take time off. Other factors considered in this study of why millennials do not take vacation time were fear of being replaced, guilt, afraid of what their boss would think, and losing consideration for a promotion. Employer communication is key. Millennials need to 1. see a corporate culture that values time off and 2. have the ability to actually disconnect during non-work hours. Otherwise, burnout will undoubtedly occur.[166]

---

166. https://projecttimeoff.com/press-releases/new-survey-millennial-attitudes-making-americas-vacation-problem-worse/

Millennial Myth: Millennials are lazy and do not want to work.

Millennial Myth—Busted: Between 2011 and 2016, 87 percent of millennials took a management position in their company in comparison with 38 percent of Gen Xers and 19 percent of boomers. As for the entrepreneurs, 54 percent of millennials either want to start a business or already have. The stereotypes don't hold up in the numbers.[167]

---

167. https://www.slideshare.net/Officevibe/20-statistics-about-millennials-in-the-workplace

CHAPTER 18

BUILDING: MODERN FAMILY

"The only rock I know that stays steady,
the only institution I know that works, is the family."

— Lee Iacocca, Former President of Ford Motor
Company and Chrysler

PUTTING FAMILY FIRST

F amilies have changed. Today's employers need to prepare for things such as same sex marriage, infertility, adoption, parental leave, day care, returning workers, and elder-care. Making certain that employees can focus on their families reduces stress and keeps workers on a more even keel. This allows them to feel supported and focused on the tasks at hand.

According to a recent article by the *New York Times*:[168]

> These kinds of benefits are a departure from the up-scale cafeteria meals, massages, and other services intended to keep employees happy and productive while at work. And the goal is not just to reduce stress for employees, but for their families, too. If the companies succeed, the thinking goes, they will minimize distractions and sources of tension that can inhibit focus and creativity.

For a shining example of a company that lives out their support of employees' families on a daily basis, we turn to **General Mills**. In 2010, the company celebrated its 15th consecutive year on the Working Mother Best Companies list. This is an honor that General Mills holds proudly and an award the company intentionally sought after. Thirty-three years ago, they set out to implement the "Best Companies" initiative with a specific focus on the needs of businesses' newest demand, the working mother. Carol Evans, the president of Working Mother Media in 2010, said on behalf of General Mills, "The immense influx of women into the workforce demanded changes in workplace culture as companies strove to keep working moms' talent and loyalty. Today, we celebrate our

---

168. http://www.nytimes.com/2012/10/20/us/in-silicon-valley-perks-now-begin-at-home.html?pagewanted=all&_r=2&

winners' untiring commitment to their employees through an impressive array of programs."[169]

As of September of 2018, General Mills found itself in the hall of fame for the 2018 *Working Mother* 100 Best Companies list yet again. Two specific company values were pointed out in the hall of fame announcement this time around: adoption benefits including up to $10,000 of reimbursement per child and employee access to a database of self-pay services like nannies, pet sitters, and housekeepers. Some categories that are represented in this coveted hall of fame include family support (reimbursement for in vitro fertilization, egg freezing, etc.), parental leave, multicultural women, and flexibility. It makes sense that 2018 marks General Mills' 23rd year on the 100 Best List.[170]

In addition to being a working mother's favorite place to work, General Mills believes in convenience for families as well. On site, you will see a hair salon, a gas station, a free medical clinic, and a concierge because they believe that those little family chores can really take time away from life. In hopes of streamlining the honey-do list, General Mills engages their employees even further by giving the option to check off that list right there at the office. Let your household eat those favorite General Mills cereals proudly.[171]

Let's look at a baker's dozen of other companies that find ways to support today's modern family.

169. https://www.generalmills.com/en/News/NewsReleases/Library/2010/September/WorkingMother

170. https://www.workingmother.com/best-companies-general-mills

171. https://groundswell.org/5-brands-with-the-best-policies-for-parents/

INCLUSIVENESS

Walgreens embraces those with disabilities. Equality is at the core of Walgreen's hiring policy. More than just serving the shareholders, it's about serving each other and the community.

The London based global tax advisory service **Ernst & Young** offers the same benefits for same-sex partners as for opposite-sex partners, even in states that don't recognize gay marriage.[172]

ADOPTION AND INFERTILITY

Wendy's offers adoptive employees a combination of up to $24,300 in adoption assistance and up to six weeks paid adoption leave.[173]

CarMax offers assistance to help Associates build families through legal adoption. Qualified associates with one year of continuous full-time service are eligible to receive up to $4,000 in reimbursements for adoption-related expenses.

The law firm **Alston & Bird** builds a $25,000 fertility benefit into employee health plans. The allowance includes coverage for treatments from in vitro fertilization to less traditional options like acupuncture.

GETTING READY FOR BABY

Facebook gives employees $4,500 when they have a baby. A welcome little bonus for the new addition.

The tech giant **AOL** helps take the stress out of being a working parent by offering fringe family benefits to employees. To start,

---

172. http://www.salary.com/14-companies-with-incredible-employee-perks
173. http://www.davethomasfoundation.org/

new moms receive prenatal instruction on everything from child-birth to newborn care through the company's Well Baby Program. New moms get eight fully paid weeks off for maternity leave.

The **University of Alberta** operates subsidized daycare facilities onsite for employees with young children and provides an offsite daycare subsidy up to $2,000 per child for employees looking for care closer to home.[174]

At **Eli Lilly,** expectant mothers are allowed to take one month of paid leave before their due date.

McMurry, a Phoenix-based marketing communications company, gives new mothers an $800 allowance for house cleaning, home health visits, meals, lactation consulting, or other services.[175]

DAY CARE

T-Mobile offers employees a childcare subsidy. According to their website, "When your life is balanced, you bring more to the job and you are better able to help our customers. That is one of the key reasons we implemented a Childcare Subsidy Program. The program is designed to help you better balance work and life. Eligible employees can receive a monthly contribution to help with childcare bills."[176]

Bain & Company offers a backup child and adult care program called Parents in a Pinch, which provides access to in-home backup child care, either temporary or ongoing, any time an employee has a gap in regularly scheduled childcare arrangements.

174. http://eluta.ca/
175. http://www.greatplacetowork.net/publications-and-events/blogs-and-news/1496
176. http://t-mobile.com/

The **McMurry** agency welcomes children at the office when day care isn't available.[177]

PARENTAL LEAVE

Aetna Life & Casualty Co. reduced resignations of new mothers by 50 percent by extending its unpaid parental leave policy to six months, saving the company one million dollars a year in training, recruiting, and hiring expenses. "The reason so many of America's top companies offer paid parental leave is that it keeps workers loyal, and that holds down turnover costs," according to IWPR President Heidi Hartmann. "It's not generosity, it's just good business."

The currency website **XE.com** offers parental leave for new fathers, paying up to 95 percent of salary for 35 weeks.

RETURNSHIPS AND MOM'S HOURS

AboutOne has a program for stay at home moms returning to the workforce. According to their website:

> Because we want to make it easier for these women to return to the corporate world, we have created AboutOne's Comeback Mom Returnship program. Similar to college internships, our Comeback Mom Returnships are for experienced professionals who want to rejoin the workforce. We offer flexible work arrangements on a trial basis to provide these 'on-rampers' with the opportunity to refine their skills and demonstrate their capabilities. Upon completion of the returnship, participants are evaluated for permanent employment with AboutOne.[178]

---

177. http://www.businessinsider.com/the-25-best-small-companies-to-work-for-right-now-2012-10?op=1#ixzz2E9AzZa51
178. http://www.aboutone.com/about-us/job-opportunities/comeback-mom-returnships/

Stew Leonard's offers "Mom's hours," enabling mothers to work while their children are in school and take off the whole summer to be with them. School delays? No problem for their work schedule.[179]

All employees at **dePoel** are eligible to work part-time or during school hours only.

SPOUSES AND KIDS

Studer Group employees receive a $75 gift card on their birthday and a $25 gift card for the birthdays of their children.[180]

Cresa Partners is an international corporate real estate advisory firm that exclusively represents tenants. They not only recognize each employee's birthday with a gift, they send spouses a gift on their birthday as well.

The oil and gas company **Anadarko** has a world-class fitness center. The center is free to employees and spouses, is open early to late and on weekends, and the company offers personalized workouts and a host of exercise classes from yoga to Zumba as well.[181]

RBA offers employees an annual allowance of "lodge credits" that can be used for the lodging portion of their family vacation.

ELDERCARE

Flexibility and team support also help employees at Houston's **Hospice Compassus**. The company recently received a special award because employee surveys consistently expressed this idea: "I feel genuinely appreciated by this company." Caring for employees who

179. https://www.indeed.com/cmp/Stew-Leonard's/reviews?fjobtitle=Cashier&start=20

180. http://www.businessinsider.com/the-25-best-small-companies-to-work-for-right-now-2012-10?op=1#ixzz2E9DclGH5

181. http://chron.com/

deal with the emotions of people facing the end of life for their family or themselves on a daily basis is important. Nurses, for example, can set their own schedules with clients. Lori Thomson, a registered nurse and executive director at the West Loop South office, says employees have access to the same bereavement workers and chaplains who work with clients. "Everybody feels for everyone else when a person is having a difficult time," Thompson said. "Hire great men and women who are talented, and treat them like family."[182]

According to **Goff Public** CEO Chris Georgacas, "We pride ourselves on being flexible to our team members' family schedules. That includes a three-month, fully paid maternity leave and "compassionate time" rather than a set number of sick hours. Compassionate time enables people to spend the time they need to with ailing family members, take good care of themselves and take care of other unexpected situations."

The Canadian Uranium producer **Cameco** provides employees with compassionate leave payments (up to 100 percent of salary for eight weeks) to workers who are called upon to care for a loved one.[183]

CustomInk, a T-shirt and apparel company based in Tysons Corner, Virginia, offers employees a dependent-care flexible spending account, which allows them to set aside $5,000 pre-tax for eldercare expenditures.[184]

182. http://chron.com/
183. http:// eluta.com
184. http://www.greatplacetowork.com/

MILLENNIAL MOMENT

Pew Research indicates that many in the millennial generation grew up with some sort of family trauma—being born to unmarried parents (25 percent) or being a child of divorce (40 percent), among other factors. However, according to a Georgia law firm, millennials are spending more time with their kids than any prior generation. The family values, despite a difference in upbringing, are still strong among millennials. While they are statistically getting married at older ages and redefining exactly what family looks like, companies that tangibly incorporate family values into their culture will attract millennials that much more.[185]

185. https://www.forbes.com/sites/jefffromm/2018/06/19/creating-meaningful-moments-for-millennial-families/#5d69666b37e1

CHAPTER 19

BELONGING: TEAM BUILDING

"The greatest predictor of a team's achievement is how the team members felt about each other. The more team members are encouraged to socialize, the more they feel connected."

— Shawn Achor, CEO and Founder Good Think

FOSTERING COMMUNITY

S uccess is frequently seen as a purely individual achievement, often at the expense of others. But in the corporate world, an organization can only thrive with the collective help of everyone. For employees, being part of a team helps create a sense of belonging. Feeling more connected leads to a greater level of happiness.

Etana is an insurance company in South Africa. The company is a market leader with a very open and unstructured culture. Etana has an interesting approach to culture. They believe in the importance of setting out values from the top, but that ultimately culture is what happens when you allow team members [Etanans] to do things. Empowerment, like a revolution (culture), starts from the bottom. Senior leadership at Etana lets employees know that they don't need buy in. In the words of the former Head of People & Culture Carel Nolte, "Don't do what we say, do what is right." The company empowers Etanans to take action and own the culture. Once they take initiative, Carel and the executive team step in with the necessary support.

Let's look at three signature examples from South Africa's Etana Insurance:

Etana is a Swahili word for "strong one." Employees [Etanans] tend not to take themselves seriously, but they take their business seriously. One team member lost a bet requiring him to run down a busy street in a speedo. In the spirit of having fun, senior leadership stepped in to raise the stakes. Employees were encouraged to join in for the run. Proceeds would go toward supporting a local men's charity. The daREDevil run is now an annual event with over 2,000 speedo-clad individuals running 4k (2.5 miles) to raise money for prostate and testicular cancer.

Etana has an in-house training department called the Etana Academy. The idea originated when a member of senior management came across an Etanan tutoring a group of fellow Etanans on a Saturday. Soon the idea of starting an accREDited learning facility was sprung. Etana now offers both online and offline courses serving Etanans, their network members, and even competitors.

The Etana REDwards applauds the efforts of those who have gone above and beyond in living the Etana values through their work. The event takes place during REDfast, a two-day getaway for all Etana staff. The awards are made by local artists and are given out to reinforce the core values at the company: **Be Open, Know, Grow, Give, and Make It Happen**. Here was a little extra that really drove home the recognition. To coincide with the event, Etana bought billboards near the home office. The billboards highlighted the different winners from the REDwards—a total surprise and delight for employees when they returned to work.

Let's look a baker's dozen of companies who actively foster a sense of community through team building.

Employees that play (music) together, stay together. **Harmonix Music Systems**, maker of the game series Rock Band, goes the extra mile to support the company's bands by providing practice space. There's a hidden sanctuary where employee bands can rock out down in the basement of their Cambridge headquarters. The dedicated practice space is equipped with stage lights, music equipment, and Christmas lights for mood.[186]

Ubermind employees sit together in small, focused teams so collaborating is an ongoing process, but the company encourages even more collaborating with competitions, lunch get-togethers, and "UberTalks—a kind of client social for the firm and guests. In the

---

186. http://www.boston.com/jobs/news/articles/2011/11/06/employee_perks_harmonix_offers_band_practice_space/

words of Brooke Walker, VP of Finance and Administration, "A lot of really good engineers want challenges. They want to work on new and exciting projects, not legacy projects."[187]

MAKE IT MEMORABLE

Decision Lens sponsors special excursions twice a year during working hours. They are completely paid for by the company. The company founder worked at several large corporations and was turned off by what he called "lame" annual company barbeques or bowling excursions. He wanted to engage his employees with group activities and trips they otherwise may not be able to on their own. For example, Decision Lens paid for its 35-person staff to visit the National Aeronautics and Space Administration's Goddard Space Flight Center about 20 miles northeast in Greenbelt, Maryland, where they listened to astronomers discuss how they've been using the Hubble Telescope. Last month, employees geared up for a day of competitive go-kart racing. According to CTO and co-founder Daniel Saaty:

> If you want to play paintball or go bowling, you can do that with your friends on your own time. The idea is to inspire people to do what they didn't think they could do. If an employee has a bad day or run of days, I want them to remember that these are the people that had his or her back and who shared an awesome, one-of-a-kind experience. That goes way beyond work.[188]

According to Rob White, CEO and co-founder of **Zeus Jones** "Most Fridays, we have what we call 'Beer and Tell,' where one or more people share [with] everyone on staff what they have been doing. The beauty of being a small company is that we can still all

187. http://adage.com/article/best-places-to-work/places-work-media-marketing-ubermind/229311/
188. http://www.entrepreneur.com/article/220512

fit in a room and celebrate the work and the little or big successes of colleagues. In addition to our work for clients, these successes include new staff welcomes, engagements, pregnancies, babies, new pets, and even winning debates with AT&T over cell phone bills. Big successes are celebrated with champagne—we write the occasion on the cork and keep all these marked corks in a jar."

HEALTHY COMPETITION

At Virginia company **Snagajob**, the Culture Squad organizes the annual Office Olympics, during which employees [Snaggers] are divided into competing nations—and dress the part.

Every four years, **Allianz** holds an international Olympics for its sports teams. The company covers the athletes' expenses and has an opening ceremony. In 2010, the games were held in Budapest with over 70 countries participating.[189]

For its hockey addicts, **PricewaterhouseCoopers Canada** hosts a unique national PwC Hockey Tournament with office teams gathering every spring for friendly competition and the chance to secure bragging rights for the year.[190]

IMPORTANCE OF PLAY AND PRANKS

It's not all work and high purpose at **OBS**. The company is big on fun. Each office has a Chief Fun Officer whose responsibility it is to ensure that fun is also an important part of the business. According to one employee, "We don't take ourselves too seriously."[191]

---

189. http://money.cnn.com/gallery/news/companies/2013/01/17/best-companies-perks.fortune/11.html
190. http://eluta.ca/
191. http://www.brw.com.au/p/sections/features/obs_takes_it_on_trust_VRWD3jsr3gF2zw1yGjqJwO

Hit them with your best shot. When things get hectic and she gets that "I just want to scream feeling" about something or someone, Jennifer Callies of **Shazaaam! Public Relations** simply opens fire. Granted it's with a Nerf gun, but the release is very gratifying. "We have a pretty small office and everyone gets along well and has a fun-loving spirit, so it was no surprise when our creative director went out one day and brought back Nerf guns for everyone," Callies says. "We take our frustrations out via Nerf wars." They shoot at walls, computers, phones, the damn copy machine and "from time to time, when the urge becomes contagious, we have it all out," she says. "It's an 'everyone for themselves' kind of war, using cubicles as hideouts and chairs as shields until all of our foam darts run out. After five to 10 minutes of heated battle with Nerf guns and childish fun, we are refreshed and ready to get back to work."[192]

Coyne PR employees work hard, but they also know how to play hard together. The agency has a practice of harmless but hilarious pranks. Previous antics included placing 200+ balloons in the cube of a vacationing employee and switching the car keys of an unsuspecting co-worker.[193]

At **McNeill Designs for Brighter Minds**, they take the time to just crack open a board game and play. "Maybe it's because we're a game development firm, but we find on a Friday afternoon, nothing beats playing a game," says CEO Donald W. McNeill. "We check out the competition and have a little healthy competition. We typically get a pizza and throw in a prize for the grand winner of the afternoon." Prizes vary from a "late morning start pass" to "party money."[194]

192. http://www.tribeinc.com/pdfs/SupplierGlobalResource_050109.pdf
193. http://www.coynepr.com/working_at_coyne.html
194. http://www.tribeinc.com/pdfs/SupplierGlobalResource_050109.pdf

OFFSITE ACTIVITIES

Each month **GoDaddy** places money toward off-site employee activities—held during work hours—to boost team morale. Recent activities for employees include whitewater rafting, gold panning, competitive cooking courses, and trapeze classes.[195]

Burton holds a Fall Bash, an annual party for Jake Burton's team, friends, and family at his home, complete with a band, food, drinks, and more. It's an annual day where the entire company hangs out together, BBQs, and has a few beers.[196]

MENTORING PROGRAMS

At **Allen & Gerritsen**, even CEO Andrew Graff has a mentor, and his mentor is the youngest person at the agency, a 22-year-old emerging-technology strategist named Eric Leist. Of course, Mr. Graff is a mentor to the strategist too. Every new employee is assigned a mentor at the Boston-area agency, but senior folks aren't supposed to do all the talking. The arrangement makes even the most junior employees "reverse mentors," so everyone knows they can learn a thing or two. According to Graff, "Don't just assume because you're more senior you're the mentor—you could be the mentee. We strive for balance. It's a young-person business; tech is taking the business in new directions, so we need to listen to the young and fearless." Mr. Graff gets schooled on why to check in to restaurants on Foursquare (for the tips) and how millennials use their phones (all the time). In turn, Mr. Leist gets sage marketing lessons from an executive with decades of experience.[197]

---

195. http://www.worldatwork.org/waw/adimComment?id=58501

196. http://mashable.com/

197. http://adage.com/article/best-places-to-work/places-work-media-marketing-allen-gerritsen/229313/

MILLENNIAL MOMENT

How can you possibly pull those millennials away from Snapchat long enough to do some team building? A Total Team Building article gives us some insight. 1. *Worthy causes.* Make your company team building good for humanity. For this very purpose-driven generation, team activities centered around a charity or a worthy cause prove to be far more engaging than the ol' trust fall. 2. *Experiences.* With unmatched access to the world's experiences with the touch of a screen, Gen Y values interactivity, experiential learning, and team building that actually holds their attention. 3. *Cross-generational mentoring.* Millennials enjoy diverse perspectives, and they have both a lot to learn and a lot to teach. Promoting collaboration among all generations in the office creates natural team building and fills the millennial mentorship bucket.[198]

---

198. https://www.totalteambuilding.com.au/how-to-engage-the-millennials-of-the-future/

CHAPTER 20

BELONGING: ATTABOYS AND ATTAGIRLS

"Teamwork is best accomplished when each team member feels valued and knows that they have a voice."

— Tom Coyne, Coyne PR

THE IMPORTANCE OF APPRECIATION

Reaching the heart of your employees involves recognition. "YOU MATTER. These two words can change your mood, change your mind, and have the power to change lives and the world if we understand and leverage them in the right way."[199] Recognition resonates in the workplace. Thirty-five percent of workers and 30 percent of chief financial officers cited frequent recognition of accomplishments as the most effective non-monetary reward. Thanking people for their hard work and commitment is key to making them feel appreciated.[200]

Stan can distinctly remember having a conversation with a law school classmate named John. John was from South Carolina. He was sharing his thoughts about his summer job working in a law office. When Stan asked if he'd considered staying on full-time after school, he shook his head, "No way." When prodded further, John revealed that he had an issue with the partner that was managing him. "He doesn't give any attaboys." Stan had never heard that word before, but no explanation was needed. John felt that his work wasn't appreciated or recognized at the firm.

Recognition fuels a sense of worth and belonging in individuals. No rocket science here, as humans we crave acceptance. Dale Carnegie spoke of the importance of recognition nearly 80 years ago. Here are a couple of quotes from his classic, *How to Win Friends and Influence People*,[201] "Be lavish in your praise and hearty in your approbation. A drop of honey gathers more bees than a gallon of gall [vinegar]."

---

199. http://www.angelamaiers.com/2011/08/new-ted-talk-you-matter.html

200. http://accountemps.rhi.mediaroom.com/index.php?s=189&item=213

201. https://www.amazon.com/How-Win-Friends-Influence-People/dp/0671027034

SHIFTING A MINDSET

Most managers take an "if, then" approach to recognition. Shawn Achor believes this paradigm needs to change "from thinking that encouragement and recognition should be used as rewards for high performance...to thinking that encouragement and recognition are drivers of high performance."[202]

Let's have a look a baker's dozen of companies who give a little extra when it comes to employee recognition.

KUDOS AND SHOUT-OUTS

Every week **The Nerdery** agency compiles a video of shout-outs with employees publicly praising their fellow nerds for going above and beyond. Five shout-out recipients are chosen for free lunches the following week. The weekly shout-out video is played for all at the Friday afternoon Bottlecap Talk, where the agency celebrates the successful launch of a recent project with a show-and-tell demo led by the rockstar developers who made it happen.

Fishbowl Fridays are held each week at **LaBreche**. Employees give kudos to each other for simple, everyday things that are done extraordinarily or out-of-the-park big hits.

BESPOKE AWARDS

According to Wellsphere, **Valtech Software** circulates a stuffed elephant for co-workers who are positive in attitude or action. The program was initiated by developer Michael Poulsen. Poulsen volunteered to be Chief Happiness Officer. Here is how he presented the program to the team:

202. https://www.amazon.com/Happiness-Advantage-Positive-Brain-Success/dp/0307591557

Purpose:
To bring all the good things we do for each other out in the light.

How it works:
The elephant is passed on from co-worker to co-worker on a weekly basis, with a reason why it is passed to that person in particular.

The reason for passing the elephant on to a new co-worker is up to you. Maybe someone helped you move apartment, fix a bug in your code, or just had a positive impact on your day by always being happy and smiling.

Ground rules for elephant care:

1. An elephant is given to a co-worker for a good reason (having a good attitude or doing something helpful).

2. The recipient must be told why he/she has been awarded the elephant.

3. The elephant can only be kept for one week, and it must be displayed for all to see.

4. Someone is in charge of the overall elephant tracking.

Rackspace created a special award for employees who give fanatical support. It's simply called The Jacket. It signifies fanaticism and hence is a straightjacket. Only one employee wins the jacket at a time.[203]

---

203. http://www.youtube.com/watch?v=iOxGVJ3Zv94

The Container Store has an award called The Gumby. Being Gumby is about doing whatever needs to be done to serve a customer, help a co-worker, or complete a task. It's about not getting "bent out of shape" when a customer makes a request of you that you'd rather not do. And it's also about bouncing back quickly after having a tough encounter with a challenging customer. Every Container Store employee is strategically trained to think flexibly to solve customer organization problems. And the company does this with an air of excitement by using the 1950s Gumby clay-figure TV star. The company constantly reinforces the Gumby culture by having a six-foot-tall wooden Gumby in the lobby at the company's headquarters and giving away the annual Gumby award to the employee who exemplifies flexibility.[204]

Decision Lens awards top-performing salespeople with custom-made action figures designed to resemble the employee. According to co-founder John Saaty, "It's a humorous way to acknowledge the great efforts of our sales team, and something that's more memorable than the usual plaque or something like that."[205]

Executives at **Zappos** pick a "hero" each month and award them with a parade, a covered parking spot for a month, a $150 Zappos gift card, and a cape.[206]

Marco distributes quarterly and annual C.A.R.E. (Customers Are Really Everything) Awards to employees who are selected by their peers for outstanding performance in teamwork, customer satisfaction, and innovative ideas. Winners receive gift packages and award certificates and recognition at Marco's annual shareholders meeting. Being employee owned also helps Marco attract and retain long-term employees who understand the relationship between the company's success and the company's customers. The "think like an

204. http://myragolden.wordpress.com/2009/04/21/how-being-gumby-can-transform-your-service-culture/

205. http://www.entrepreneur.com/article/220512

206. http://www.youtube.com/watch?v=q2hMA22Jlfc

owner" attitude of employees is demonstrated through the long-term relationships they've developed with clients over the years.

At social game and advertising company **RockYou**, good ideas are recognized every six weeks with the YouRock Awards hosted at the company's all-hands meetings. The YouRock Awards started as a way to promote a bottom-up employee nomination process so people could recognize those with whom they work daily. Driven by peer nominations, RockYou awards teammates for solving a problem, designing a game, demonstrating innovation, and exhibiting behaviors aligned with the RockYou values. YouRock nominees spin a wheel to choose an award such as cash, concert tickets, an extra day off, or an iPad. All YouRock recipients also receive a Golden Bobble-head Cow trophy, offering them desktop bragging rights. The open forum in which people can be recognized and recognize others fosters a compassionate and playful company culture.[207]

The coveted peer-nominated Water Carrier award at **CamelBak** is presented annually to a group of employees who uniquely embody and transfer company culture and values to other associates. The award is named in honor of the Native American tradition of carrying water to fellow tribe members to sustain life and provide one of the essential elements for survival.

The **Tabar** Thumbs Up Award is a roaming statue that sits on an employee's desk when he or she goes over and above the call of job performance.

Martin | Williams gives out an annual award called The Ribble, which is a trapeze term for a great catch, something the audience just expects. It goes to people who day-in and day-out come to work and do such a good job that people really come to depend on them

---

207. http://mashable.com/2011/08/07/startup-employee-perks/

in ways that almost blind them to their importance. They represent the best of our culture.

You may not need to wear formalwear to pick it up, but if you're caught doing great work at **Undertone**, you may win an "Undertonie." It's just one way the digital advertising company encourages and rewards creativity. There are also weekly massages, manicures, and a free-beer cart.[208]

IMMEDIATE RECOGNITION

Each **SC Johnson** office has a Now Thanks! Program. The program provides on-the-spot recognition for great work with praise and a monetary award.[209]

American Express has a Prize Patrol. A group of four or five leaders get together and surprise their coworkers with flowers or a gift in front of their colleagues to celebrate their accomplishments.[210]

TAKE NOTE: THE BEST THINGS IN LIFE ARE FREE

A research study confirmed that the cost of recognition awards has only minimal impact on employee perception of appreciation. Fifty-seven percent reported that the most meaningful recognition was free. Just look at some of these quotes to judge the impact:

- "I received a handwritten thank you in the mail from my manager and my CEO. I smiled like an idiot." - Bill A.

208. http://adage.com/article/special-report-best-places-to-work-2012/undertone-9-ad-age-s-places-work-list/233652/

209. http://www.businessinsider.com/the-25-best-places-to-work-around-the-world-2012-11?op=1#ixzz2E8vD2ohm

210. https://www.businessinsider.com/the-25-best-places-to-work-around-the-world-2012-11?op=1#ixzz2E8wKdZqw

- "I got a bonus with a handwritten note. I read the note several times; even took a picture of it. Bonus was good, too, but [I took] no picture." - David H.

"Because few people expect much in the way of reward these days, a small but personalized thank you can have a big impact," says Steve Richardson, founder of **Diverse Outcomes** and former chief talent officer for American Express. "Even when I send a recognition note to a big group or team, I try to add a personalized paragraph in each person's email, so it's highly tailored to the individual."[211]

Former CEO of the **Campbell Soup Company** Doug Conant is a big proponent of the power of handwritten notes. In Doug's words:

> Look for opportunities to celebrate. My executive assistants and I would spend a good 30 to 60 minutes a day scanning my mail and our internal website looking for news of people who have made a difference at Campbell's. Get out your pen. Believe it or not, I have sent roughly 30,000 handwritten notes to employees over the last decade, from maintenance people to senior executives. I let them know that I am personally paying attention and celebrating their accomplishments. (I send handwritten notes too because well over half of our associates don't use a computer). I also jump on any opportunities to write to people who partner with our company any time I meet with them. It's the least you can do for people who do things to help your company and industry. On the face of it, writing handwritten notes may seem like a waste of time. But in my experience, they build goodwill and lead to higher productivity.[212]

---

211. http://blogs.hbr.org/hbr/hewlett/2012/05/attract_and_keep_a-players_wit.html
212. http://blogs.hbr.org/cs/2011/02/secrets_of_positive_feedback.html

The managing partner at **Windes & McClaughry Accountancy** actually handwrites all employee welcome, birthday, and anniversary cards. He also gives a red rose to women employees and cookies to men employees on Valentine's Day.

Plan B Technologies attributes its success to going the extra mile for clients, and it does the same for staff. Employees enjoy fully paid health-care premiums, an $85 monthly contribution to a health savings account, regular telecommuting, quarterly awards, spot bonuses, frequent free meals, and handwritten thank you notes from the CEO.[213]

Long before he became CEO of **iProspect**, back as an analyst at Bain Capital and KPMG, Robert J. Murray had an idea on how you should run a services business. "One thing that always surprised me in prior work experiences is when your assets walk out the door each day, why aren't companies doing more to value the people doing the business?" Mr. Murray thinks he's found the answer to that, and quite a large number of his employees happen to agree. Mr. Murray's formula: hire competitive people; promote early and often; give constant feedback, including iProps—notes of encouragement. "We are a meritocracy. When positions come open, we don't care if you've been here six months or six years—we will promote the best person into that position," he said.[214]

Thank you Thursdays at **Professional Placement Resources** fosters a culture of gratitude that extends to clients as well. On Thank you Thursdays, the CEO asks employees to send a specific number of thank you notes to both internal and external customers.

---

213. http://washingtonian.com/

214. http://adage.com/article/best-places-to-work/places-work-media-marketing-iprospect/229326/

RECOGNIZING MILESTONES

The tenure program at **Sweetgreen** called Shades of Green has blown up into a competition and become a status symbol among employees. Every teammate gets a free shirt, and the longer you're with Sweetgreen, the darker your shirt. Who knew a free t-shirt could help to shape company culture? After teammates have been with Sweetgreen for one year, they also get a pair of green high-top Converse sneakers. At two years, they get a t-shirt and a neon green iPod Nano Touch. After three years, they get a lime-green Sweetgreen bike.[215]

Clif Bar was born on a bike. Every employee in the company received a bike on the 20th anniversary of the company.

My close friend told me about her friend's first week working at **O Magazine**. In addition to being an awesome gig, she got a $10,000 check and an iPad on her second day there. I first assumed that it was a good sign-on bonus; however, she explained that it was not. Rather, it was just incredible timing; it was a one-time thank you gift Oprah gave to all the staff regardless of how long they had been with the company.[216]

As we all know, millennials have been receiving their recognition high on social media for years now, so companies employing this generation will really have to step up their game. Flackable has figured out a way to attract and retain its millennial workers. On day one of the job, the new hires get welcomed to the team with a new hire press release. After the first day jitters are over, employees are encouraged to contribute to blog posts, articles, and more so they can continually have a way to receive that recognition they love.[217]

---

215. http://mashable.com/2011/08/07/startup-employee-perks/

216. http://flavors.me/bwelfel

217. https://www.inc.com/brian-hart/how-promoting-your-company-can-help-you-attract-retain-top-millennial-talent.html

Every significant anniversary at the **St. Regis Hotel** is acknowledged with a party, a plaque, and a gift from Tiffany.[218]

Employees at **Harbinger Partners** receive a gift each month. CEO Scott Grausnick has distributed gifts that range from a Harbinger umbrella to flowers to iPads to big-screen TVs. "It's just really, really nice," said Cindy Smith, Harbinger's finance administrator. "It's so much fun to get some mail. It's all about the little things they think of."[219]

The **Hotze Health & Wellness Center** gives employees a piece of Waterford crystal to mark key accomplishments and anniversaries. Every new employee, including accountants and publicists, must pass an exam on the first try that shows they understand the entire treatment regimen at the clinic. "It's stressful, especially for those who aren't used to the medical terminology, so Hotze likes to recognize the accomplishment with a piece of crystal from Waterford," said Christy Hammett, assistant director of public relations and marketing. "Each staff member gets two more pieces— typically wine goblets or Champagne flutes—one at the annual Christmas party and on their yearly anniversary they receive another." Patterns are assigned based on availability. Founder and CEO Steven Hotze, a longtime fan of Waterford crystal, wanted to give his employees something they'd treasure and pass down through the generations, said Hammett, who has amassed six or seven Champagne flutes in the Elberon pattern. Hammett says she brings them out when she entertains, as she did earlier this year to toast her engagement. "I didn't even register for crystal," she said. "I'm getting that at work." The perk began 21 years ago and impresses job applicants as well. "They get so excited when they get the first one."[220]

---

218. http://chron.com/

219. http://bizjournal.com/twincities

220. http://www.chron.com/business/top-workplaces/article/Paid-volunteer-time-dogs-at-work-and-other-perks-2254147.php

Brady, Chapman, Holland's diamond program encourages generosity in daily work life. When a BCH employee does something exceptionally well for a client, fellow employee, or the community, an acrylic diamond is tossed in a jar. Once the jar fills up, they celebrate by playing a game or going to a sports bar.[221]

LAGNIAPPE: Roger Staubach once said, "There are no traffic jams on the extra mile." How about this example of going "above and beyond" to help an employee? One of the agency principals at **Mantis Pulse Analytics** was alerted that an employee was having major car issues. He went on Craigslist and bought a transmission. He towed the employee's Jeep to his house and fixed it.

MILLENNIAL MOMENT

Everybody gets a trophy. It is no mistake that millennials have been called "the participation trophy generation" due to a massive wave of parents and coaches wanting every child to be included and feel an equal part of the team. Lauren can tell you from experience that her childhood room in her parents' home is still filled with trophies from dance, volleyball, academics, and the like, ranging from first place to participation awards. Companies must keep in mind that this generation has lived their entire lives receiving attaboys and attagirls from their superiors, so, of course, they will expect the same amount of praise and encouragement in the workforce. According to Aon Hewitt, 38 percent of millennials would like to see the current recognition program at their office improved.[222]

---

221. http://chron.com/

222. https://ir.aon.com/about-aon/investor-relations/investor-news/news-release-details/2015/Aon-Hewitt-Study-Reveals-Nearly-Half-of-Millennials-Intend-to-Pursue-New-Jobs-in-2015/default.aspx

Millennial Myth: Millennials have been coddled and entitled due to the participation trophy epidemic and now require hand-holding at work.

Millennial Myth—Busted: What if those participation trophies had a reverse effect? The Society for Diversity explains in their blog that because this generation was exposed to constant affirmation from their superiors, it has created a need to impress their leaders at work. We can see this theory proven in the data that tells us millennials are the least likely to take vacation days and, when they do, they end up still working either for fear of disappointing their boss or just losing their job altogether. Perhaps excessive trophies have created workaholics as opposed to entitled individuals.[223]

---

223. http://www.societyfordiversity.org/millennials-and-the-participation-trophy-mindset/

CHAPTER 21

BELONGING: FLEXIBILITY

*"It's not just the number of hours we sit at a desk
that determines the value we generate.
It's the energy we bring to the hours we work."*

— Tony Schwartz, CEO of The Energy Project

TAKING CONTROL

F lexibility is about control, and everyone wants flex. According to the Center for Talent Innovation's research, if there's one work perk that rises above the rest, it's flexible work arrangements. The CTI study showed that 87 percent of boomers, 79 percent of Gen Xers and 89 percent of millennials cite flex as important.[224]

Why be flexible? The bottom line benefit for companies is increased productivity and job satisfaction. According to Sylvia Ann Hewlett:

> Companies that treat time as currency—through remote work options, staggered hours, and reduced-hour arrangements—are also more likely to attract and retain high-caliber employees. Work/life balance has always been prized by working women juggling the demands of family and high-powered jobs, and now these moms are being seconded by incoming Millennials, who consider it a basic entitlement to play as hard as they work.

A CHANGING WORKPLACE

By some estimates, perhaps one-quarter of all U.S. jobs could be performed remotely, and in a 2011 survey of 2,000 U.S. businesses, one-quarter of them said they planned to use more remote workers in the future.[225] Forty percent of U.S. workers have jobs that could be done from home at least part of the time.[226] It›s already happening. Regular telecommuters at Cisco and Accenture exceed 80 percent of their workforce. Many tech experts are convinced we won't even need offices as we know them in the future.[227]

---

224. http://www.worklifepolicy.org/
225. https://www.mckinseyquarterly.com/Preparing_for_a_new_era_of_knowledge_work
226. http://www.teleworkresearchnetwork.com/
227. http://money.cnn.com/magazines/fortune/best-companies/2012/benefits/telecommuting.html

WORKSHIFTING BY THE NUMBERS

Citrix has pioneered the concept of **Work·shift·ing**. Work·shift·ing is using the web to get work done anytime, anywhere—outside the traditional office space. It produces savings for employees, employers, and the environment:

- Workplace flexibility can save employers up to $20,000 per employee per year.

- Workshifters save between $4,000 and $21,000 per year in travel and work-related costs.

- 80 percent of employers say workshifting options help recruit talent.

- Companies with telework policies realize an 18 percent savings in real estate, electricity, and office expenses.

- Half-time telecommuting nationwide would spare the environment the equivalent of taking 10 million cars permanently off the road.

Increasing business performance and employee satisfaction

- Workshifters are 55 percent more engaged than non-workshifters.

- When telework policies are introduced, companies report a 25 percent reduction in employee attrition.

- Workshifting increases productivity by 27 percent.

- 72 percent of employees say flexible work arrangements would cause them to choose one job over another.

- Turnover for employees who do not have the flexibility is almost twice the rate of those who do.[228]

Let's look at a baker's dozen of companies who push the limits of flexibility.

Patagonia Inc., based in California, attracts outdoorsy types with its athletic clothing brand and laser-like focus on work-life balance. "Time away from the office isn't just tolerated here, it's required," says Rob BonDurant, Patagonia's Vice President of Marketing and de facto culture guide. Its 1,300 employees enjoy what the company calls "Let My People Go Surfing" time—a period during any work day where employees can head outdoors to get their creative juices flowing. Of course, they can't abandon their duties or ditch a meeting, but popping out for an impromptu climb or bike ride is encouraged. Patagonia's flextime policies, which originated from Yvon Chouinard, an outdoor enthusiast who founded the company in 1974, are good for employee morale and invaluable to the company. In the words of BonDurant, "The time we spend outside the office helps us manage the storytelling process around our products. We're designing ski and surfing apparel, we need to be traveling and trying things out."[229] Patagonia also gives employees two weeks of full-paid leave to work for the green nonprofit of their choice.[230]

228. http://citrixonline.com/
229. http://entrepreneur.com/
230. http://inc.com/

CONTROL OF HOURS / SCHEDULE

Managers struggle to judge employees on outcomes, not hours, since defining clear goals and determining reasonable timelines are difficult.

According to **JetBlue**'s VP of Talent Bonny Simi, "Bosses need to just relax. They don't have to see the employee for the work to get done. That's the hardest shift in mindset for some managers. They [employees] don't want to work 9 to 5—and it doesn't matter to me if they work better from six at night until three in the morning or if they can do the work in six hours instead of eight."

Work schedule flexibility is a major reason employees prefer working at **Busch Gardens**. It has helped make the Tampa Bay theme park a go-to employer. According to David Bode, VP of Human Resources, "We learned how to be very flexible because we employ a lot of students with strange hours and people who rely on us for second jobs. Plus, our work demand varies so much." Busch needs a minimum of 1,500 people to keep the place open seven days a week. They bulk up the staff to 4,500 for the peak summer and winter seasons between Christmas and Easter. But needs vary dramatically with weather, the day of the week, the time of day, and attendance projections, so the park has made schedule juggling an art form. "It's great," said Chris Noyce, a 21-year-old USF environmental sciences major in his third year as a ride operator. "When you work is almost up to you." Employees post their availability on a company website. Shifts are pared down to work units of four to six hours. The computer matches available employees to attendance projections and work demands two weeks ahead of time. The supervisors then fine-tune and juggle the actual work assignments—even down to the same day.[231]

---

231. http://www2.tbo.com/

At **Brand Learning,** directors are trusted to manage their time and way of working, within reason, and there are reduced work options of two and a half, three, and four-day weeks.

Believe it or not, **Point B**, a Portland management consulting company, offers its employees no paid vacation time or holidays—and the employees seem to love it. That's because this company believes so firmly in flexibility that associates get paid only for the time they work, so there is no arbitrary limit to how much time off they can take. "I've never worked anywhere that was as committed to helping employees realize what the work-life balance means to them individually," says one employee.[232]

The furniture retailer **IKEA** offers a range of alternative work options to help employees balance work-life commitments, including flexible hours, shortened and compressed work week options, and job-sharing arrangements.

Lori Ames at **ThePRFreelancer.com** has a small business with two employees. In her words, "One of my employees is dating a New York City police officer, who works five days on, two days off, five days on, three days off. I've structured her schedule so that she works the same days as he does and is off for two days each time he's off. Sometimes her weekend is Monday and Tuesday, sometimes Saturday and Sunday; but it's made for a very happy employee."[233]

REMOTE ACCESS

All employees at **Fulcrum Inquiry** receive a laptop computer plus remote access to all of the firm's technology and files. All employees can work remotely if their particular assignment at that time makes

---

232. http://www.oregonbusiness.com/articles/112-march-2012/6795-the-2012-list-top-33-small-companies-to-work-for-in-oregon?start=3#ixzz25HAskUmS
233. http://theprfreelancer.com/

this practical. All employees occasionally work remotely. A few employees work extensively from home and during non-standard hours. Workers also boast a flexible schedule. Consultants own their schedule based on client needs.

Flexibility is the norm at accounting firm **PricewaterhouseCoopers** (PwC). With more than 160,000 employees operating in 154 countries, PwC has one of the highest percentages of telecommuters with 70 percent of employees working from home at least 20 percent of the time.

Netflix believes that hard work is not relevant. According to CEO Reed Hastings:

> We don't measure people by how many hours they work or how much they are in the office. We do care about accomplishing great work. Sustained B-level performance, despite "A" for effort, generates a generous severance package, with respect. Sustained A-level performance, despite minimal effort, is rewarded with more responsibility and great pay.

Jeff Gunther, CEO of the Charlottesville, Virginia, based **Meddius**, a software company, decided he would change the way his staff works by instituting a Results Only Work Environment (ROWE). Meddius employees can work any time from any place in any way, as long as they get their work done. Gunther has found that by giving employees the trust and autonomy they need, they've actually been more productive and loyal to the company.[234]

Edmunds.com boasts an innovative corporate culture, highlighted by a rollout of a Results Only Work Environment in 2012. Under ROWE, Edmunds.com employees are offered the freedom to work

---

234. http://www.inc.com/guides/2010/08/10-things-employees-want.html

at any time from any location where they can most effectively deliver their expected results.

In the words of Matthew DiGeronimo, Principal at **Smith Floyd**, "I enforce NO work hours. [We are] performance driven—not hours logged driven. Employees can even attend staff meetings from home (via Skype) if they desire."[235]

PERKS/CONCIERGE

At **SC Johnson**, 12,000 employees have access to a concierge service that will take care of just about any chore from returning overdue library books to making sure your dry cleaning gets picked up on time. The Wisconsin based company is in the business of cleaning products after all.[236]

During the firm's busy season, a perk plan is offered at **RBZ, LLP**. It includes weekly manicures, massage therapy, daily catered dinners, nightly office-wide Trivial Pursuit games, an espresso cart, and free hotel stays nearby. A full-time concierge runs errands, and a free house cleaning each three-month season rounds out this incredible benefit.

Benefits are first class at **Counterpart International Inc.** In addition to health insurance and a 403(b) fund, the organization offers three lifestyle benefits (employees choose one): gym membership, a $125 public transportation benefit, or paid parking in the building's garage.[237]

235. http://smithfloyd.com/
236. http://www.thefiscaltimes.com/Articles/2011/05/19/16-Company-Perks-That-Will-Make-You-Jealous.aspx#qcvJOSjM6q3jBsqP.99
237. http://www.prnewsonline.com/

JOB ROTATION

Employees at **MERS/Missouri Goodwill Industries** can try on various positions for the best fit.

"Orionites," as they call themselves at **Orion Trading**, don't like to stay in one place. The company encourages employees to try different jobs from time to time, moving in and out of marketing, sales, client services, or media investment. The goal is to grow employee skills, which Orion has found increases everyone's output.

WORKING OFF-SCRIPT

From a post by Jay Baer at Convince & Convert:

> Mid-way on a **Southwest Airlines** flight home from a speaking engagement in Ft. Lauderdale, I looked up from my laptop to find Becky the flight attendant standing at the front of plane with a boy of about nine. 'Ladies and gentlemen, I'm sorry to disturb you, but I just thought you should know that we have a celebrity on the plane today. Well, perhaps not a celebrity today, but someday this young man will be a famous artist. Abraham has drawn us a marvelous picture. It's quite wonderful, and I'll be displaying it up here so we all can enjoy his great picture.' The kid was absolutely BEAMING with pride and accomplishment and happiness and honor. Abraham returned to his seat. Becky broke out the medical kit, ripped open a band-aid and used it as ersatz tape to post the picture on the wall. A few minutes later, Abraham was back with a second picture. A landscape this time, Becky again made an announcement and grabbed another band-aid.

When I talk about focusing on BEING social, rather than focusing on DOING social media, this is what I mean. Social business isn't about tools and technology. It's about giving Becky the freedom to work off-script. It's about cultural DNA that values moments of delight. It's about treating customers as humans, not transactions. It's about winning hearts and minds one planeload at a time with a personal, shared experience. And it's about building loyalty and triggering word-of-mouth by doing it well. Will Abraham's parents ever fly any other airline? Will he? Will I? Or you?[238]

FLEXIBILITY WITH KIDS

Schools Financial Credit Union (SFCU) allows any of its employees to bring their newborns to work until the child is six months old. According to the Vice President of Marketing at the company, the babies cause little distraction, and since the parents can continue performing most of their work duties, the company doesn't have to hire temps or train new people.[239] **SFCU** also supports a program called School Activities Leave. Employees may take off up to 40 hours per year for participation in a child's school activity.

Hot Studio worked closely with the Parenting in the Workplace Institute, a non-profit based in Salt Lake City, Utah, to create their Babies-at-Work program. The Institute helps organizations start successful programs, and it maintains a growing database of more than 140 workplaces around the country that allow babies at work. Baby-inclusive organizations report higher morale and retention, increased teamwork, an easier transition back to work for new parents, enhanced client loyalty, and greater interest from job ap-

---

238. https://purplegoldfish.com/outcomes-not-hours-flexibility-is-becoming-a-mandate-for-employee-engagement/
239. https://www.mamamia.com.au/bring-babies-to-work/

plicants. According to Principal, Program Planning and new Mom Courtney Kaplan, "Dividing my life into separate roles at work and at home is stressful. It's nice to have a program at Hot that offers a more integrated choice. The office is the new village."

Hot Studio has implemented a structured, formal Babies-at-Work policy with specific provisions to ensure that all employees' needs are taken into account and that the babies are not disruptive to the efficient functioning of the company. The agency views its babies-at-work program in line with its other programs that accommodate employee volunteer interests and other family needs. Especially in these difficult economic times, Hot Studio is proud to offer a program to its employees that eases the substantial burden of high infant day care costs and the all-too-common—and grueling—situation in which parents must separate from their newborn babies at a few weeks or months of age to return to their jobs.

In the words of Hot Studio's CEO and founder, Maria Giudice, "I managed to grow a company and raise two children of my own in the 13 years of being in business. I brought my babies to work until they were each eight months old and I'm happy to see other new mothers doing the same. We are proud and thrilled to be affiliated with the Babies-at-Work Program."[240]

Here's another brilliant creative move by Hot Studio. The company has purchased a soundproof booth to serve the dual purposes of a quiet space for parents to take fussy babies as needed and, when parents and babies aren't using the booth, a place for video sound editing for client projects.

240. http://www.hotstudio.com/thoughts/hot-studio-welcomes-babies-work-new-pilot-program

FLEXIBILITY WITH PAY AND BENEFITS

All employees at **Darden** Restaurants (Red Lobster, Olive Garden, LongHorn Steakhouse, The Capital Grille, Bahama Breeze, Seasons 52, and Eddie V's) are eligible for health insurance and disability coverage from the first day of employment, which is highly unusual in the restaurant business. In addition, Darden pays employees on a weekly basis, rather than bi-weekly—even though it costs them more to do so—because they recognize the economic needs of their workers.

Unlike many technology and management consulting companies, **Jabian Consulting** focuses on local client engagements, meaning its consultants do not endure the typically grueling travel demands that often come with consulting work.

FLEXIBLE DRESS CODE

Several winning workplaces stress the importance of the right atmosphere. At **BBS Technologies** that means striving to replicate the freedom and intellectual excitement of a college campus. CEO Rick Pleczko said he wants everyone to feel comfortable at the software company as he tries to combine a casual atmosphere with a professional environment, "We care what you produce and deliver, but not so much how you look,"[241]

---

241. http://www.chron.com/business/top-workplaces/article/Paid-volunteer-time-dogs-at-work-and-other-perks-2254147.php

MILLENNIAL MOMENT

Flexibility over finances. That's right, HubSpot shows us that 45 percent of millennials would choose work flexibility over pay any day.[242] Truthfully, all generations are desiring more flexibility in their work hours and locations according to a 2018 NBCNews article but, as usual, millennials take the cake. NBC sheds light on a study that found the sweet spot for employee engagement for millennials was to work offsite 60-80 percent of the time, or 3-4 days per week.[243] While this may seem foreign to certain businesses and industries, optimal engagement means significant productivity. Just ask the millennials which coffee shop in town has the best WiFi.

242. https://cdn2.hubspot.net/hubfs/1999999/mini-guides/pdf/statistics-about-millenials.pdf

243. https://www.nbcnews.com/better/business/7-ways-millennials-are-changing-workplace-better-ncna761021

CHAPTER 22

BELONGING: RETIREMENT

"Preparation for old age should begin not later than one's teens. A life which is empty of purpose until 65 will not suddenly become filled on retirement."

— Arthur E. Morgan, Civil Engineer,
U.S. Administrator, and Educator

LIFE AFTER WORK

Retirement benefits can be a driver of engagement. How can you help employees plan for and be prepared for the next stage of life? Let's look at a handful of companies that go the extra mile to prepare and take care of employees for life after work.

BIG CONTRIBUTIONS

Devon Energy is an oil and gas explorer and producer. They have developed a new 401(k) retirement plan allowing for annual company contributions of a whopping 11 to 22 percent.

GSM, an IT consultancy in Leesburg, Virginia, has big perks, including five weeks of vacation, a 401(k) contribution of 15 percent of salary, fully paid health-care premiums, $1,200 toward the creation of a will, $5,000 a year to attend training or conferences, $720 toward Internet access, and $1,750 toward the purchase of a gadget—although employees are given all the technology they need for their jobs.[244]

PLANNING, PHASING, PREPARING

TD Bank helps employees plan for life after work with retirement planning assistance. The program includes a defined benefit pension plan, matching contributions to a share purchase plan, and a health benefits plan that extends into retirement with no age limit.[245]

DIALOG is a multidisciplinary firm comprised of architects, engineers, interior designers, and urban designers and planners. The firm helps older workers prepare for retirement with contributions

244. http://washingtonian.com/
245. http://eluta.ca/

to a matching RSP plan and phased-in work options that allow employees to gradually leave the workforce.

The **University of Toronto** offers a phased-in retirement work option for those nearing the end of their careers. They also help employees prepare for life after work with retirement planning assistance services along with generous contributions to a defined benefit pension plan.[246]

British Columbia Safety Authority provides phased-in work options that allow employees to gradually leave the workforce and health benefit coverage that extends to retirees.[247]

MILLENNIAL MOMENT

Student debt is expensive and typically takes the spotlight over saving for retirement according to Douglas Boneparth, author of *The Millennial Money Fix,* in a *CNN Money* article. Paying off student loans is an enormous weight that many millennials have to take on. In 2018 alone, the outstanding student loan debt in the U.S. is 1.5 trillion according to stats from the Federal Reserve. Employers must recognize that, more than likely, their Gen Y employees do not have much room in their head or bank account to intentionally save for retirement. Giving them the option to save through work benefits is an ideal situation for them.[248]

246. http://eluta.ca/
247. http://eluta.ca/
248. https://wtop.com/local/2018/07/money-is-on-our-minds-millennials-attempt-to-stay-afloat-amid-student-loan-debt/

CHAPTER 23

BECOMING: TRAINING AND DEVELOPMENT

"Learning at Accenture is changing people's lives; it's giving them more reason than ever to stay with us and grow both personally and professionally."

— Jill Smart, Accenture

ESTABLISHING A CULTURE OF LEARNING

Investing in your employees involves training and development. Let's look at a baker's dozen of companies that go the extra mile to allow employees to learn how to become the best version of themselves.

Evernote has a program called Officer Training. CEO Phil Libin got the idea from a friend who served on a Trident nuclear submarine. His friend said that in order to be an officer on one of these subs, you have to know how to do everyone else's job. Those skills are repeatedly trained and taught. In Phil's words:

> And I remember thinking, 'That's really cool.' So we implemented officer training at Evernote. The program is voluntary. If you sign up, we will randomly assign you to any other meeting. So pretty much anytime I have a meeting with anyone, or anyone else has a meeting with anyone, very often there is somebody else in there from a totally different department who's in officer training. They're there to absorb what we're talking about. They're not just spectators. They ask questions; they talk. My assistant runs it, and she won't schedule any individual for more than two extra meetings a week. We don't want this consuming too much of anybody's time.[249]

Chicago-based online advertising buyer **Centro LLC** focuses on the manager-employee relationship. Centro spends a lot of time training managers. Why? Because people quit bosses, not jobs. The biggest reason employees leave is because of their managers. Scott Golas, vice president of human resources, says his company focuses on the manager-employee relationship. "Let's face it: People leave companies because of their boss," Mr. Golas says. "We try to re-

---

249. https://www.nytimes.com/2012/04/08/business/phil-libin-of-evernote-on-its-unusual-corporate-culture.html

move the typical obstacles (between bosses and employees) by sharing more information, by providing great training and by making
sure those bosses have the right skill sets."[250]

A recent study by Assocham revealed about 70 percent of [survey]
respondents said that employees who quit their jobs complain about
the indifferent attitude of their bosses or immediate supervisor.

Want to increase employee engagement? It's not "brain surgery."
The single biggest driver is the quality of the relationship with the
employee's direct manager. Put an emphasis on developing managers of people.

Gallup interviewed 10 million employees around the world. They
asked them the following question: "Would you agree with this
statement, 'My supervisor or somebody at work, cares about me as
a person?"

Those who agreed

- were more productive.

- made greater contributions to profits.

- were more likely to stay with the company long
  term.[251]

Ecumen's Velocity Leadership program is a major way Ecumen
honors and empowers achievement. Each year up to 25 emerging
leaders are selected for a very thought-provoking leadership development program that includes visits to other innovative companies
to learn from them, guest speakers on innovation and leadership,
and other learning and personal growth opportunities. It allows

250. http://www.chicagobusiness.com/article/20120331/ISSUE02/120329728/why-your-perks-arent-working#ixzz23eQnmYWN

251. https://www.amazon.com/Happiness-Advantage-Principles-Psychology-Performance/dp/0307591549

employees to step outside of their daily work and lives and focus on their individual growth as a person and leader.[252]

Squeeze In, a group of California and Nevada restaurants, has an annual 3-day off-site management retreat called Format. According to Eva Lipson:

> "We get all our Managers and Owners together to review reports and numbers, discuss management styles, refresh our techniques, review our menu, and hear suggestions to make it better, and most importantly bond and team build. We encourage self-development and management growth by offering up books to read (including *Purple Goldfish*) and then we have them write short book reports. When they turn in their book reports, they get a cash bonus. This year we had a number of books on their list to read, and when they finished them all (and wrote reports on each), we presented them with free iPads! Also, during the 3-day retreat, we take them out to eat at restaurants (always interesting for a group of servers to go out and be served), and imbibe in a few cocktails too. We know that our Format retreat increases camaraderie, reinforces our company culture and helps with employee retention. It's a great way for us to show our Managers how much we love them and care about them, both professionally and personally."[253]

TRAINING AS A COMPETITIVE DIFFERENTIATOR

Colliers founded Colliers University (CU) in 2002. It was truly a novel concept within the commercial real estate industry. Built on

---

252. http://www.9inchmarketing.com/wp-admin/www.bizjournals.com/twincities/
253. http://www.squeezein.com/

the premise that learning can be a competitive advantage, CU has grown to include more than 1,000 classes and has helped accelerate the professional and personal success of thousands of Colliers professionals. The curriculum offers a 360-degree approach to learning with courses in commercial real estate, business, and personal development.

CU is not only a culture driver for the company internally, it is an outwardly competitive recruitment tool, raising the bar in terms of the expertise of their professionals. This expertise directly benefits clients through better results and memorable experiences."[254]

MyLearning, the global online learning portal for **Accenture**, boasts 20,000 learning courses that range from core training to technical training. Accenture Learning BPO Services and Accenture work together today to annually serve more than 125,000 learners through more than 200,000 classroom learning days and more than 1,000 virtual learning sessions. The team discovered that for every dollar Accenture invests in learning, the company receives that dollar back plus an additional $3.53 in measurable value to their bottom line—in other words, a 353 percent return on learning. According to Jill Smart, Senior Managing Director of Human Resources at Accenture, "Learning at Accenture is changing people's lives; it's giving them more reason than ever to stay with us and grow both personally and professionally."[255]

The Container Store puts an emphasis on training. Employees receive on an average 160+ hours of training per year. Typical annual turnover in retail is 100 percent, but at Container Store, it hovers around 15-20 percent.[256]

---

254. http://www.colliers.com/TrainingandDevelopment

255. https://mylearning.accentureacademy.com/lms/courses

256. http://www.achievemax.com/blog/2009/03/12/the-container-store/

Wegman's, a popular grocery store chain that started in upstate New York, offers employees two to three times more training than other grocery stores. In turn, turnover at the chain is only seven percent compared to 19 percent industry-wide.[257]

TUITION REIMBURSEMENTS AND MORE

Hoar Construction puts an emphasis on personal and professional development. Employees receive up to $10,000 in annual tuition reimbursement, plus Hoar offers employees a variety of courses through their internal university ranging from money management and stress reduction to tips on building a nonprofit.[258]

Boeing pays for college degrees pertinent to position and provides stock awards for degree completion.[259]

Monsanto encourages ongoing employee development with generous tuition subsidies (up to $10,000), financial bonuses for some course completion, and subsidies for professional accreditation.[260]

STAYING CURIOUS AND CURRENT

Nina Hale strives to create a culture of curiosity and passion, even going out of its way to encourage employees to share information with each other. As part of that push, the company hosts weekly "shared education" meetings where an employee picks a topic to discuss. "There's a lot of new and different skill sets, so each person brings a new area of expertise to the table," Senior Account Manager Leslie Gibson said. "Everyone's willing to share what they've learned, and no one ever makes anyone else feel stupid."[261]

---

257. http://www.customerbliss.com/
258. greatplacetowork.com
259. https://www.glassdoor.com/Reviews/Employee-Review-Boeing-RVW65538.htm
260. http://eluta.ca/
261. http://www.bizjournals.com/twincities/

One program at **Automation Direct** is called Wake Up and Learn. Four times a year, the company hosts a variety of speakers to discuss personal and professional development topics including budgeting, managing stress, and healthy eating.[262]

Horizon Media has introduced the Knowledge Café, an educational series inviting media and tech executives to talk to employees and clients. Recent speakers include Hulu CEO Jason Kilar and Pandora CEO Tim Westergren. "We program our space in a way that's meaningful to employees. We're always trying to figure out how to stay current with the evolution of the business, but in a timeless way."[263]

VISUAL THINKING

Twice a month for two hours, employees at **XPLANE** meet to discuss various topics of personal and professional interest and work on collaboration, storytelling, and presentation skills. "The Visual Learning School is about using pictures to help people better think about complex issues, solve problems, and communicate more effectively," says XPLANE creative director Matt Adams. "The most valued result is team building and the strengthening of relationships through learning, spontaneity, and improvisation."[264]

262. http://www.entrepreneur.com/article/220512

263. http://adage.com/article/special-report-best-places-to-work-2012/horizon-media-10-ad-age-s-places-work-list/233649/

264. http://www.entrepreneur.com/article/220512

MILLENNIAL MOMENT

Training and development is a hot commodity for the working millennial. Here are some numbers from the eLearning Industry website: 1. Millennials rated professional growth and development as the number one factor in engagement and retention in Quantum Workplace. 2. Roughly 35 percent of Gen Yers believe excellent training and development programs are crucial when considering a potential employer. 3. Seventy-two percent of millennials rank the chance to learn new skills as valuable alongside 48 percent of boomers and 62 percent of Gen Xers. Millennials have been exposed to learning and developing through their fingertips since they were very young. It makes sense that they have a high regard for self-improvement and proficiency. Employers that value growth value the millennial worker.[265]

---

265. https://elearningindustry.com/millennial-workforce-7-key-ld-strategies-shouldnt-miss-engage

CHAPTER 24

BECOMING: PAYING IT FORWARD

*"From what we get, we can make a living;
what we give, however, makes a life."*

— Arthur Ashe

GIVING BACK

Embracing purpose and giving back to society are strong drivers of employee engagement. The ability for employees to be part of something that is larger than themselves is immensely gratifying. You can't talk about the concept of paying it forward without mentioning TOMS and Blake Mycoskie. They are championing the idea that a company can sell a quality product, be profitable, and give back to those in need.

Here's the story of how the company was founded. In 2006, Blake took some time off from work to travel to Argentina. He was twenty-nine years old and running his fourth entrepreneurial startup. Besides learning the tango, playing polo, and drinking Malbec, Blake got used to wearing the national shoe: the alpargata. The alpargata is a soft, casual canvas shoe worn by almost everyone in the country: in the cities, on the farms, and in the nightclubs. He wondered briefly if the alpargata would have some market appeal in the United States, but he was taking time for enjoyment, not work, while he was in Argentina. Before leaving Argentina, Blake met an American woman in a café who was volunteering at a shoe drive. She explained that many kids lacked shoes, even in relatively well-developed countries like Argentina. The lack of shoes made it difficult to attend school or to go to the local well for water. It also exposed the children to a wide range of diseases, blisters, and sores. Her organization collected shoes from donors and gave them to kids in need. The problem was their total reliance on donations meant shoes were not always available or available in the needed size. That meant even if there were shoes, a child could still be shoeless because none of them fit. After traveling with her for a few days and then traveling on his own, Blake begin to think about a solution in the direction of entrepreneurship, not charity. He decided to create a for-profit business to help provide shoes for these children. TOMS was the result. The purpose of TOMS is to use business to improve lives and pay it forward.

The company was founded on a model that matched every pair of shoes purchased with a new pair of shoes for a child in need. The program is called "One for One®." TOMS has given over 86 million pairs of shoes to children in need. The shoes are always given to children through humanitarian organizations who incorporate shoes into their community development programs. The One for One concept has spread from shoes. TOMS Eyewear was launched in 2011 and has helped give sight to over 600,000 people in need. TOMS Roasting Co., launched in 2014, has helped provide over 600,000 weeks of safe water. With each purchase of TOMS Roasting Co. Coffee, Giving Partners provide 140 liters of safe water (a one-week supply) to a person in need. The TOMS purpose "to use business to improve lives" is amply carried out by the expanding and very effective One for One® program with the buy one, give one philosophy.

Let's look at a baker's dozen of companies that go the extra mile to enable employees to serve those in need.

LETTING EMPLOYEES GIVE BACK

Umpqua Bank allows its employees to give back to the community. Here is a comment by employee Heather Primeaux. "We are given and encouraged to use 40 hours of paid time each year to volunteer, which I can and do use to volunteer at my kids' schools and for field trips."[266]

Volunteering is part of public relations firm **MWW**'s ethos. MWW created Matter More Day to give all employees the opportunity to volunteer for their favorite non-profit organization. On this day, all offices close for one day of company-wide volunteering. The MWW Citizen of the Year Award is presented at the end of each year to one employee who has made an outstanding contri-

266. http://money.cnn.com/magazines/fortune/bestcompanies/2011/snapshots/25.html

bution to improving his or her community. The award includes a sizable donation made in the winner's name to the charity of their choice. MWW programs include: Tools for School (MWW offices collect supplies for distribution to low-income and foster children); Neighbor to Neighbor (MWW kicks off the holiday season by helping food banks in its communities to obtain, prepare, and distribute Thanksgiving meals for families in need); Letters to Santa (MWW makes wishes come true for hundreds of children in the communities where it works.)[267]

VOLUNTEERING PLUS A LITTLE EXTRA

Embrace Home Loans has the Embrace Cares program. The Newport based company offers 100 hours of paid time off per year for volunteering and donates $10 for every hour worked by the employee to the volunteer organization of their choice.[268]

Employees at **National Rural Electric Cooperative Association** are encouraged to volunteer. For every 24 hours of time an employee gives to charity, he or she receives an extra vacation day.[269]

QBP gives $10 to any 501(c)3 organization for every hour up to 40 hours a year that QBP employees volunteer there.[270]

GIVING BACK AND DONATING

Microsoft donated $844 million worth of software to nearly 47,000 nonprofits in 2011. The Oregon office has an annual

267. http://www.prnewsonline.com
268. http://greatplacetowork.com/
269. http://washingtonian.com/
270. http://outsideonline.com/

giving campaign where employee contributions are matched dollar-for-dollar.[271]

Northrop Group, a global security group, was recently voted as the number one best place to work according to millennials. Why do ages 22-38 love working here? Because of their social impact initiatives including STEM education, veteran's services, and environmental and natural disaster response.[272]

Decision Analytics Corporation, a military contractor, believes in giving back. Each quarter, staffers assemble care packages for soldiers overseas.[273]

The employees of Canadian airline **WestJet** manage a highly focused charitable program through an in-house Community Investment Team. They support numerous initiatives every year and donate close to 5,000 flights to charitable initiatives yearly.[274]

LENDING SKILLS AS WELL AS HANDS

Hewlett Packard empowers employees to make a difference and give back. Employees are encouraged to give 4 hours a month to community or give-back work. Here's some interesting math: 4 hours per month x 300,000 employees = 1,200,000 hours of HP social impact.[275]

The Olympics are close to the heart of the people running and working for **Lane4**. The company takes its name from the swimming lane given to the competitor with the fastest heat. The firm advises other businesses and human resources leaders on organizational

271. http://www.oregonbusiness.com/articles/112-march-2012/6794-the-2012-list-top-34-medium-companies-to-work-for-in-oregon
272. https://www.cnbc.com/2018/06/19/the-10-best-places-to-work-according-to-millennials.html
273. http://washingtonian.com/
274. http://eluta.ca
275. http://hp.com/

change, leadership development, and executive coaching. Adrian Moorhouse, who won swimming gold at Seoul, set up Lane4 with a leading sports psychologist in 1995 to show that people can achieve excellence in everything they do if they have the right "high-performance" environment. They practice what they preach. The business contributes to the community in Bourne End, Buckinghamshire, by running a free walk-in clinic on CV [resume] writing and interviewing techniques to help tackle local unemployment.[276]

SPONSORSHIP

Tabar fully sponsors a child in each full-time employee's name through the organization Save the Children. Tabar currently sponsors 23 children worldwide. Employees also get paid time off for approved volunteer work for community or church services.[277]

GOING ABOVE AND BEYOND

Knight Point Systems founded by a service-disabled veteran, has donated more than $106,000 to charity over the last three years. In addition, the management team buys lunches or dinners for service-members they see in airports.[278]

In 1986, **Patagonia** committed one percent of sales or 10 percent of pretax profits, whichever was greater, to local NGOs committed to fighting for the environment. In the last 30+ years, the company has given tens of millions of dollars back to the environment.[279]

---

276. http://www.thesundaytimes.co.uk

277. http://outsideonline.com/

278. http://washingtonian.com/

279. https://www.patagonia.com/one-percent-for-the-planet.html

MILLENNIAL MOMENT

"Despite negative stereotypes about millennials, our survey research shows that savvy millennials are raising the most charity-conscious generation in history." That quote came from Art Taylor, President and CEO of Give.org. This generation is raising the next generation to give it all back as best as they can. Millennials themselves only account for about 11 percent of charitable donations which, at first glance, makes them look really bad. But when we look closer at an article by Jason Notte for TheStreet, we see that 84 percent of the generation participates in charity giving. The story the data paints is that, even though millennials are giving less, more members of the generation give than any other generation. Additionally, this generation is willing to give more than money by donating clothes, talents, and time. Perhaps this has something to do with the 7.2 percent unemployment rate for ages 20-24 and the average of about $37,000 of student debt per college graduate according to the Bureau of Labor Statistics and Cappex.com. America as a country is giving less than they ever have before yet the millennial generation is not following the trend. If you want to keep millennials in the company, give them not only the option but the company policy to do what they thrive doing: giving.[280]

280. https://www.thestreet.com/story/14445741/1/why-millennials-are-more-charitable.html

CHAPTER 25

BECOMING: EMPOWERMENT

"Life is work, and work is life, and both are a struggle. It's doing meaningful work and being valued for it—not picnics—that makes it all worthwhile."

— Vineet Nayar, CEO of HCL Technologies

TAKING CONTROL

L eadership is about inspiring others. It's enabling team members to do their absolute best to work toward a meaningful and rewarding shared purpose. In one word—EMPOWERMENT. Help people find their direction, support them with resources, and then get out of their way.

Maybe one of the strongest examples of empowerment is **Nordstrom**. Their entire mission and employee handbook fit on a business card:

> FRONT SIDE: Nordstrom has only one goal, "To provide outstanding customer service."

> BACK SIDE: We have only one rule, "Use good judgment in all situations."

IT'S TIME FOR A CHANGE

Command and Control or Carrot and Stick thinking is outdated. People do not enjoy or appreciate being controlled or coerced.

The best managers figure out how to get great outcomes by setting the appropriate context rather than by trying to control their people.[281]

According to Ken and Scott Blanchard, "We are finding that giving people a chance to succeed in their job and setting them free to a certain degree is the key to motivation, as opposed to trying to direct and control people's energy. It's really about letting go and connecting people to their work—and each other—rather than channeling, organizing, orchestrating, and focusing behavior."[282]

---

281. http://www.slideshare.net/reed2001/culture-1798664

282. http://www.fastcompany.com/3002382/why-trying-manipulate-employee-motivation-always-backfires

Let's look at a baker's dozen of companies that go the extra mile to empower team members.

EMPOWERMENT IS THE OPPOSITE OF ORGANIZATION

W. L. Gore was founded by Wilbert Lee Gore in 1958. A 16-year veteran at DuPont, Bill envisioned a different type of organization. His organization would be non-hierarchical, setting an environment where leaders would emerge based on the merit of their ideas.

> [Gore] wanted a company where employees' spirit grew based on what they accomplished, not which corporate scrimmage they had won—where more time was spent generating ideas than generating ways to cover one's backside. So, he decided to create a "non-organization" approach for his new company that would inspire creativity in its employees.[283]

LIFE COACHES AND DREAM MANAGERS

Zappos provides a life coach for employees.[284]

Infusionsoft provides employees with the services of a "Dream Manager." The move was inspired by Matthew Kelly's book *The Dream Manager* and fulfills a core value at Infusionsoft. The sales and marketing automation provider believes in people and their dreams. The manager works to help team members set, pursue, and become accountable for achieving their goals and dreams.[285]

---

283. http://chiefcustomerofficer.customerbliss.com/2013/01/08/do-your-employee-ideas-see-the-light-of-day/

284. http://www.youtube.com/watch?v=701MOt3_qCk

285. http://culture.infusionsoft.com/preserving-the-core/how-do-you-hire-a-dream-manager/

The commercial developer **Brasfield & Gorrie** created a new position, Director of Career Development. The move is paying dividends. The company maps out each employee's career path and indicates what he or she will have to do to get there. "Every employee's career path is consistent with what we're looking for from our strategic plan five to 10 years out. We're not just making something up." Spelling out every employee's career path takes time and part of that time is spent making sure upper management communicates the results with individual employees.[286]

SUPPORTING PERSONAL GOALS

Associates at **Pepsico** include a personal goal in their performance development review process and are asked to deliver against this goal, just like any other goal, to ensure a work-life balance.[287]

Following the opportunity to take time to evaluate where the associate is now, and where he or she wants to be, each team member at **Falgren Mortine** then meets with his or her supervisor for a conversation. At least one hour is devoted to focusing on the individual's needs and goals and a chance to formally discuss ways he or she can grow and learn in the development of his or her career.[288]

TITLES NEED NOT APPLY

This leading developer empowers everyone to make a personal mark on the company and culture. According to Mike Derheim, CEO at **The Nerdery**:

> "We want them to aspire to be a co-president. The late great Luke Bucklin was the only president we'll ever have, and

---

286. bizjournals.com/atlanta/

287. http://www.businessinsider.com/the-25-best-places-to-work-around-the-world-2012-11

288. http://www.prnewsonline.com

co-president was what he called us—all of us—before we lost him. In one of Luke's last all-staff emails he wrote: 'Put your business card on the desk in front of you. Look at it. ... This card does not define you. You are a **Co-President**. You are bigger than your defined role. ... Play your part—transcend your job title, be a hero."[289]

Matt DeGeronimo at **Smith Floyd** sent us this message: "I run a Mergers & Acquisitions company in Honolulu and had some thoughts for your book. There is one thing we do that might not be commonplace. We allow employees to pick their own title. Creative titles encouraged."[290]

The independent marketing agency **WONGDOODY** is united by the Democracy of Good Ideas principle. Any staffer could come up with the next big idea. It encourages participation and rewards keen judgment.[291]

PURPOSEFULLY LOSING CONTROL

One of Europe's leading manufacturers and suppliers of single-use medical products, **Molnlycke Health Care** allowed production teams to decide how to meet their goals. With the responsibility for quality products moved to individuals on those teams, nearly 70 percent of the company's new products launch on time compared with just 15 percent previously. As a result, the company will have quadrupled its shareholder value in only five years.[292]

289. http://www.bizjournals.com/twincities/

290. http://smithfloyd.com/

291. http://www.labusinessjournal.com

292. http://www.innovation.lv/ino2/publications/leonardo_manual/en/www.innosupport.net/webhelp/wso/index.cfm@fuseac-tionlearnl_id4287pl_id3561.htm

PASSIONS AND THE CREATIVE MUSE

Fast Horse is an innovative, integrated agency offering a full range of traditional and non-traditional marketing services. Fast Horse employees enjoy little extras like Muse It or Lose It, a $500 stipend to help underwrite creative endeavors away from the office.

Much of the credit for creating an amazing workplace at **Weber Shandwick Minneapolis** goes to their Employee Action Group (EAG). Each month, employees enjoy an EAG-sponsored event to celebrate their successes, encourage teamwork, or to just have fun. The highlight events include the annual "Shank-wick" golf outing and their own version of "The Amazing Race," appropriately renamed "The Shan-mazing Race." The newest EAG initiative is their "No Boundaries" program. This program was designed to give their employees a chance to explore a personal passion, which could include attending "The Burning Man" event in San Francisco to spark creativity or traveling to Honduras to work for Soles4Souls, a non-profit organization devoted to distributing shoes and clothing to victims of abject suffering. The company provides the employees with five extra vacation days and $1,000 to pursue the passion.[293]

MAKING TIME FOR EMPOWERMENT

3M launched the 15 percent program in 1948. Employees were given 15 percent of their time to work on a personal project of their choosing. If it seems radical now, imagine how it played as post-war America was suiting up and going to the office with rigid hierarchies and increasingly defined work and home roles. But it was also a logical next step. Forty plus years in the red taught 3M a key lesson: **Innovate or Die**, an ethos the company has carried dutifully into the twenty-first century.

---

293. http://www.bizjournals.com/twincities/

15 percent time is extended to everyone. Who knows who'll create the next Post-It Note? (a 15 percent time innovation) "It's one of the things that sets 3M apart as an innovative company, by sticking to that culture of giving every one of our employees the ability to follow their instincts to take advantage of opportunities for the company," says Technical Director Kurt Beinlich, who tries to get most of his 70-person lab team to participate.[294]

Azavea, a maker of mapping software, lets employees spend up to 10 percent of their time on research projects of their own devising.

HACK DAYS AND THE QUEST FOR IMPROVEMENT

Conductor, Inc. holds an annual, company-wide Hack Day, where all Conductors are invited to self-organize into teams and spend a day developing an idea that makes the product, office, or company better.[295]

Siemens operates an employee suggestion program that encourages employees to share their feedback. The ideas that lead to savings or new revenues are evaluated for their impact and can lead to financial bonus payments ranging up to $100,000.

Employees at **McMurry** can submit their innovative WOW Project ideas through the company's internal computer network. Toward the end of the year, president and CEO Chris McMurry and several senior managers consider each of the hundreds of pitches that come in and award up to $10,000 for the best ideas. "Our business, and every business, needs to innovate constantly if it seeks an enduring future," McMurry says, explaining why the program got started. One winning pitch came from a group of three employees who pored over U.S. Post Office regulations and came up with a

---

294. http://www.fastcodesign.com/1663137/how-3m-gave-everyone-days-off-and-created-an-innovation-dynamo
295. http://greatplacetowork.com/

way for McMurry to re-sequence how it distributes mail on behalf of its clients, saving those clients millions of dollars.

Encouraging its staff of more than 170 people to dream up creative business ideas and solutions has cemented innovation into our culture," McMurry says. "It's now part of what everyone does. It has put all my colleagues in a continuous improvement mode. There literally isn't a week that goes by where someone doesn't implement a better way of doing something."

R&D THURSDAYS

Nearly every employee at **Spider Strategies** works from home every day. Staffers set their own hours—which suits those who prefer to work at night. There are rarely meetings—three or four a year. Every Thursday is set-aside for R&D, so staffers can explore the latest in technology. And vacation is unlimited.[296]

THE ABILITY TO CORRECT MISTAKES

Starbucks will fix your drink if it's wrong, every time—no charge. Starbucks employees are empowered to provide drinks on the house for repeat customers when they are having a bad day, out of money, or "just because." Crewmembers spend a day during their first week of training simply going out into the lobby and greeting customers. The goal is not just to ask them what they need or provide a refill, but to actually engage in conversation and help the person become more comfortable while waiting or relaxing. Crewmembers are empowered to provide "service recovery certificates" for a free "anything" (even a quad-venti five pump caramel macchiato, light whip, hold the foam) when service fails to meet the customer's expectations.

---

296. https://www.washingtonian.com/2011/11/01/50-great-places-to-work-in-washington/

Tellers at **Fairwinds Credit Union** are empowered to provide immediate service recovery of up to $100 per incident without seeking management approval. This can be used to buy a customer lunch, purchase flowers, send a special treat, or for anything else the employee decides would help recover from a bad service experience.

EXHIBITION AND SCIENCE FAIRS

Practice Plan, which provides business support services to the dental sector, gets the creative juices flowing among its workforce of 74 people by giving in-house exhibition space for original artwork every two months. Darren Marks used his turn to show a series of nine images called Words To Live Your Life By, based on song lyrics. Colleagues shared drinks and nibbles at the opening of his "Wall 9" exhibition.

Once a year, about 200 employees from dozens of divisions at **3M** make cardboard posters describing their 15 percent time project as if they were presenting volcano models at a middle school science fair. They stand up their poster and then hang out next to it and await feedback, suggestions, and potential co-collaborators. Wayne Maurer, an R&D manager in 3M's abrasives division, calls it a chance for people to unhinge their "inner geek." He elaborates, "For technical people, it's the most passionate and engaged event we have at 3M."[297]

---

297. http://www.fastcodesign.com/1663137/how-3m-gave-everyone-days-off-and-created-an-innovation-dynamo

MILLENNIAL MOMENT

Contribution. It takes one word to sum up what millennial employees want. This generation has been liking, sharing, retweeting, and commenting on social media channels for years and has grown quite used to being able to voice their opinion. Since middle or high school, they have had the option to put in their two cents. Giving your millennial employees the ability to work on their own ideas, provide feedback when necessary, and contribute to projects they care about is not an office perk but a real necessity. As of May 2018, *Forbes* delivered the news that 4,500 out of a surveyed 10,500 millennials are planning on leaving their jobs within two years. How do you keep them around? Give them autonomy. Ask for their opinion. Let them contribute to world good through their company. Also, stop calling them millennials. They hate that.[298]

---

298. https://www.forbes.com/sites/zackfriedman/2018/05/22/millennials-quit-job/#27b41f8a57f1

PART IV:

FINAL THOUGHTS

CHAPTER 26

FIVE MAIN TAKEAWAYS

We hope you enjoyed the book and that it has made you think—and possibly reassess a few things. Here are five final points for you about Green Goldfish:

YOU CAN'T MAKE CHICKEN SALAD ...

You can't make chicken salad out of chicken shit. Creating Green Goldfish is not a substitute for having a strong product or service. Hire the right people, compensate them fairly, and allow them to do meaningful work. Get the basics right before giving the little unexpected extras.

AUTHENTIC VS. FORCED

A Green Goldfish is a beacon. A small gift or offering that demonstrates you care. Why do we love our parents? It's because they loved us first. Green Goldfish need to be given in an authentic way. If it comes across as forced or contrived, you'll eliminate all of the goodwill and negatively impact your culture.

A DAILY REGIMEN OF EXERCISE VS. LIPOSUCTION

A Green Goldfish is not a quick fix or for those seeking immediate results. Translation: it's not liposuction. It's equivalent to working out every day. Culture gradually builds and improves over time.

IT'S A COMMITMENT, NOT A CAMPAIGN

A Green Goldfish is different than a one off or limited offer. Add one or a school of Green Goldfish at your convenience, but remove them at your peril.

EVERY GREAT JOURNEY BEGINS WITH A SINGLE STEP

Start small when adding a signature extra and add more gradually. Remember the concept of Trojan Mice. The best brands are those who boast a whole school of Green Goldfish for their employees.

ADDITIONAL INSPIRATION AND FURTHER READING

Let My People Go Surfing, The Education of a Reluctant Businessman - Yvon Choinard

Influence - Robert Cialdini

Touchpoints - Doug Conant

Peak: How Great Companies Get Their Mojo from Maslow - Chip Conley

Uncommon Service - Frances Frei and Anne Morriss

The Power of Moments - Chip Heath and Dan Heath

Ownership Quotient - James L. Heskett, W. Earl Sasser, Joe Wheeler

Delivering Happiness: A Path to Profits, Passion, and Purpose - Tony Hsieh

Dream Manager - Matthew Kelly and Patrick Lencioni

Employee First, Customers Second - Vineet Nayar

Purple Goldfish: 12 Ways to Win Customers and Influence Word of Mouth – Stan Phelps

Golden Goldfish: The Vital Few - Stan Phelps

Drive: The Surprising Truth About What Motivates Us - Daniel Pink

StrengthsFinder 2.0 - Tom Rath

Why Work Sucks & How to Fix It: No Schedules, No Meetings, No Joke – Cali Ressler and Jody Thompson

Maverick: The Success Story Behind the World's Most Unusual Workplace - Ricardo Semler

The Seven Day Weekend - Ricardo Semler

ABOUT THE AUTHORS

STAN PHELPS

Stan Phelps is a best-selling author, keynote speaker, and workshop facilitator. He believes that today's organizations must focus on meaningful differentiation to win the hearts of both employees and customers.

He is the founder of PurpleGoldfish.com. Purple Goldfish is a think tank of customer experience and employee engagement experts that offers keynotes and workshops that drive loyalty and sales. The group helps organizations connect with the hearts and minds of customers and employees.

Prior to PurpleGoldfish.com, Stan had a 20-year career in marketing that included leadership positions at IMG, adidas, PGA Exhibitions, and Synergy. At Synergy, he worked on award-winning experiential programs for top brands such as KFC, Wachovia, NASCAR, Starbucks, and M&M's.

Stan is a TEDx speaker, a Forbes contributor, and an IBM Futurist. His writing is syndicated on top sites such as Customer Think and Business2Community. He has spoken at over 300 events across Australia, Bahrain, Canada, Ecuador, France, Germany, Holland, Israel, Japan, Malaysia, Peru, Russia, Singapore, Spain, Sweden, UK, and the U.S.

He is the author of eight other business books and one fun one:

- *Purple Goldfish - 12 Ways to Win Customers and Influence Word of Mouth*

- *Golden Goldfish - The Vital Few*

- *Blue Goldfish - Using Technology, Data, and Analytics to Drive Both Profits and Prophets*

- *Purple Goldfish Service Edition - 12 Ways Hotels, Restaurants and Airlines Win the Right Customers*

- *Red Goldfish - Motivating Sales and Loyalty Through Shared Passion and Purpose*

- *Pink Goldfish - Defy Ordinary, Exploit Imperfection, and Captivate Your Customers*

- *Purple Goldfish Franchise Edition - The Ultimate S.Y.S.T.E.M. for Franchisors and Franchisees*

- *Yellow Goldfish - Nine Ways to Drive Happiness in Business for Growth, Productivity, and Prosperity*

- *Bar Tricks, Bad Jokes, & Even Worse Stories*

Stan received a BS in Marketing and Human Resources from Marist College, a JD/MBA from Villanova University, and a certificate for Achieving Breakthrough Service from Harvard Business School. He is a Certified Net Promoter Associate and has taught as an adjunct professor at NYU, Rutgers University, and Manhattanville College. Stan lives in Cary, North Carolina, with his wife, Jennifer, and two boys, Thomas and James.

Stan is also a fellow at Maddock Douglas, an innovation consulting firm in Chicago.

To book Stan for an upcoming keynote, webinar, or workshop, go to stanphelpsspeaks.com. You can reach Stan at stan@purplegoldfish.com or call +1.919.360.4702 or follow him on Twitter: @StanPhelpsPG.

LAUREN MCGHEE

Lauren is the CEO and owner of Lauren McGhee Coaching and is a Gallup-certified StrengthsFinder coach and speaker. Her core belief is that everyone should thrive in their design.

Lauren works with executives through individual coaching focused on the relationships between their top strengths and their leadership style. She also leads team development sessions with a concentration on strengths-based partnerships, the DNA of the team, and how to use individual and team strengths in action to promote increased employee engagement.

Through keynotes, workshops, facilitations, and trainings, Lauren speaks on the topics of living and working with a strengths-based mindset, defying "well-rounded thinking," and millennials in the workplace. Lauren also has a "just for fun" keynote detailing her hilarious recount of getting married to her husband in the middle of Hurricane Matthew in 2016.

Lauren graduated with a B.S. in Entrepreneurship and Business Development from the University of North Carolina at Wilmington. She now lives in Wilmington, NC with her husband, Tyler, and their 8-year-old mutt, Samantha.

To book Lauren for an upcoming keynote, webinar, or workshop, go to laurenmcoaching.com. You can reach Lauren at lauren@laurenmcoaching.com or call +1.910.340.3772.

OTHER COLORS IN THE GOLDFISH SERIES

Purple Goldfish – 12 Ways to Win Customers and Influence Word of Mouth. This book is based on the Purple Goldfish Project, a crowd-sourcing effort that collected more than 1,001 examples of signature-added value. The book draws inspiration from the concept of lagniappe, providing 12 practical strategies for winning the hearts of customers and influencing positive word of mouth.

Golden Goldfish – The Vital Few: All Customers and Employees Are Not Created Equal. Golden Goldfish examines the importance of your top 20 percent of customers and employees. The book showcases nine ways to drive loyalty and retention with these two critical groups.

Blue Goldfish - Using Technology, Data, and Analytics to Drive Both Profits and Prophets. Blue Goldfish examines how to leverage technology, data, and analytics to do a "little something extra" to improve the experience for the customer. The book is based on a collection of over 300 case studies. It examines the three R's: Relationship, Responsiveness, and Readiness. *Blue Goldfish* also uncovers eight different ways to turn insights into action.

Red Goldfish - Motivating Sales and Loyalty Through Shared Passion and Purpose. Purpose is changing the way we work and how customers choose business partners. It is driving loyalty, and it's on its way to becoming the ultimate differentiator in business. *Red Goldfish* shares cutting edge examples and reveals the eight ways businesses can embrace purpose that drives employee engagement, fuels the bottom line, and makes an impact on the lives of those it serves.

Purple Goldfish Service Edition - 12 Ways Hotels, Restaurants, and Airlines Win the Right Customers. *Purple Goldfish Service Edition* is about differentiation via added value. Marketing to your existing customers via G.L.U.E. (giving little unexpected extras). Packed with over 100 examples, the book focuses on the 12 ways to do the "little extras" to improve the customer experience for restaurants, hotels, and airlines. The end result is increased sales, happier customers, and positive word of mouth.

Pink Goldfish - Defy Ordinary, Exploit Imperfection, and Captivate Your Customers. Companies need to stand out in a crowded marketplace, but true differentiation is increasingly rare. Based on over 200 case studies, *Pink Goldfish* provides an unconventional seven-part framework for achieving competitive separation by embracing flaws instead of fixing them.

Purple Goldfish Franchise Edition - The Ultimate S.Y.S.T.E.M. For Franchisors and Franchisees. Packed with over 100 best-practice examples, *Purple Goldfish Franchise Edition* focuses on the six keys to creating a successful franchise S.Y.S.T.E.M. and a dozen ways to create a signature customer experience.

Yellow Goldfish - Nine Ways to Drive Happiness in Business for Growth, Productivity, and Prosperity. There should only be one success metric in business and that 's happiness. A Yellow Goldfish is any time a business does a little extra to contribute to the happiness of its customers, employees, or society. Based on nearly 300 case studies, *Yellow Goldfish* provides a nine-part framework for happiness-driven growth, productivity, and prosperity in business.